August Strindberg

This book is due on the last date stamped below.
Failure to return books on the date due may result
in assessment of overdue fees.

A Smith and Kraus Book
Published by Smith and Kraus, Inc.
PO Box 127, Lyme, NH 03768

Cover and Text Design by Julia Hill Gignoux, Freedom Hill Design
Cover Illustration: The Isle of the Dead by Arnold Böcklin

First Edition: March 2000
10 9 8 7 6 5 4 3 2 1

The Library of Congress Cataloging-In-Publication Data
Strindberg, August, 1849–1912.
[Plays. English. Selections]
August Strindberg : five major plays / translated by Carl. R. Mueller. —1st ed.
p. cm. — (Great translations series)
Contents: The father — Miss Julie — The stronger — A dream play — The ghost sonata.
ISBN 1-57525-261-9
1. Strindberg, August, 1849–1912—Translations into English. I. Title: Five major plays.
II. Mueller, Carl Richard. III. Title. IV. Great translations for actors series.
PT9811.A3 M84 1999
839.72'6—dc21 99-089191

August Strindberg

FIVE MAJOR PLAYS

Translated by Carl R. Mueller

Great Translations Series

SK
A Smith and Kraus Book

FOR
HUGH DENARD

Contents

INTRODUCTION

The Swedish playwright August Strindberg (1849–1912) remains almost a century after his death one of the most important western playwrights on the world stage, a man of letters whose enormous output is staggering for its variety, and an essential factor in the history of the development of the modern theater.

THE HISTORICAL CONTEXT

August Strindberg, playwright, novelist and short-story writer, spent all but a relatively short period of his life as a full-time writer, though he practiced other disciplines in which he demonstrated considerable proficiency— painter, photographer and amateur chemist.

Strindberg's life was anything but peaceful and contented. It was, in fact, seldom less than a nightmare, and frequently much worse. He flirted with insanity several times in his life, and the question is still open on whether he ever descended into that mental condition. He went, for example, through a period in the 1880s in which he suffered profound psychological and spiritual upheaval. It was in this period that he wrote three of the plays in this collection: *The Father* (1887), *Miss Julie* (1888), and *The Stronger* (1888–89)— plays whose plots and incidents fed off of the turmoil of their author's own life and personal relationships. These were plays written in the naturalist mode of the time, the movement in the arts spurred on by the revolutions in science, the advent of Darwin, the historical and political observations of Marx, and the manifestoes of Émile Zola. In theater and literature there were the Goncourt brothers, Balzac, and in particular André Antoine, the founder in 1887 of the influential experimental theater known as the Théâtre-Libre, which first introduced Strindberg to Paris.

He was married three times, each time to a professional woman: Siri von Essen, a middling actress; Frida Uhl, an Austrian journalist; and Harriet Bosse, a highly talented Norwegian actress. But each of these marriages caused him mental and physical torment, instigated largely by his own mental problems and personal idiosyncrasies. It is these torments that informed most of his naturalistic work in the theater, as well as in such works as *The Red Room* (1879), a *roman à clef,* and *Married* (1884), a collection of short stories. All three of his wives wrote of their lives with him, providing a remarkably detailed and informed account.

Strindberg's relationship with Sweden was almost as turbulent as that with his wives. He had little success in his native country until fairly late in his life. The disaffection caused him to abandon Sweden and live abroad in Switzerland, Germany, Austria, Denmark, and France—Paris being the most important and necessary conquest for any serious artist. From 1889 onward, at least five major Strindberg plays were performed there, several of them at Antoine's Théâtre-Libre. But it was in Germany that his greatest success abroad was realized.

His "exile" had begun in 1882 and ended with his return to Sweden in 1896, and with that return he began a series of some of his most famous and influential plays. It has been called his "expressionist" period, although expressionism as a movement did not formally begin until 1905 in Germany, and in the German theater not until 1910. In retrospect, however, Strindberg's "expressionist" plays were fully realized examples of the movement-to-come.

His plays of this period are experimental in the most profound way. As he says in his Author's Note to *A Dream Play:* "Characters split, double, and multiply; they evaporate, crystallize, dissolve, and reconverge." The dream became for him the insubstantial bedrock of theatrical truth. "Anything can happen, everything is possible and probable. Space and time do not exist. Based on a slight foundation of reality, imagination wanders afield and weaves new patterns comprised of mixtures of recollections, experiences, unconstrained fantasies, absurdities, and improvisations." It is of historical interest to note that the other great experimenter with dreams, Sigmund Freud, published *The Interpretation of Dreams* in Vienna in 1900, one year before the composition of *A Dream Play.*

Strindberg's expressionist experiments began as early as 1898 in *To Damascus I* and ended in 1909 with the pilgrimage play *The Great Highway.* Within those dates he wrote two more parts of *To Damascus,* plus *A Dream Play* and *The Ghost Sonata.* Within this period, too, he also wrote a great sequence of more than twenty historical plays based on Swedish history and written in the form of the chronicle play, the best examples of which are *Master Olof* (1872, first version), *Erik XIV* (1899), and *Gustav Adolf* (1903).

One of Strindberg's final contributions to the theater of his time was to cofound with August Falck a new kind of theater for Stockholm in 1907: the

Intimate Theater. He had been profoundly influenced by Max Reinhardt's theater-space experiments in Berlin at the turn of the century, the Kleines Theater (Little Theater) and the Kammerspiele (Chamber Theater). Like them, the Intimate Theater was a small space in which actors could act like people rather than like larger-than-life-size creatures in the relatively vast spaces of city and state theaters. Emotions in this new theater were to be conveyed in an intimate way, a smile or raised eyebrow was to take the place of a speech or a large gesture. Actually he had been writing "intimate" plays long before the establishment of the Intimate Theater, as, for example, *Miss Julie* and *The Stronger*. But in anticipation of the opening of the Intimate Theater he wrote a flight of what he called his "chamber plays," all in 1907, of which *The Ghost Sonata* is one.

Strindberg has been called "the playwright's playwright," perhaps because he poured out a vast stream of plays that emerged as if from a state of possession, as if playwriting were his lifeline. Some of these plays are cornerstones in the history of western theater, many are quite good, and perhaps even more than half are of little importance, but none are less than artistically provocative. Along with Ibsen, Strindberg is one of the earliest voices of modernism in world drama, perhaps a better term is "modern consciousness," because of his psychological acuteness. He is, as Thornton Wilder has said, the source of everything that is modern in drama, and anticipated the dilemma of modern man. Strindberg was one of the forerunners of the so-called "theater of the absurd," a fanatic experimenter who, as Sean O'Casey so insightfully declared, "shook down the living stars from heaven." Strindberg was a quintessentially distraught individual who used his talents and passions to explore the "enigmas of the universe as well as those of dramatic form."

THE PLAYS

THE FATHER

The power of the will is not an unknown factor in Strindberg's scheme of things; it appears in several of the plays in this collection, but is most prominent in *The Father*. Much is made of the Captain's weakness of will and of his wife Laura's strength of will. Laura tells the Doctor that the Captain no sooner makes a decision than he has repudiated it, and she avers that she scorns him for that. But will is precisely what has been the dominant factor in Laura during her twenty years of marriage to the Captain. The current struggle between them has to do with the upbringing and education of their daughter Bertha. Laura wants her to be raised at home under her supervision; the Captain wants her boarded out and educated in town where she will be free of her mother's excessive influence, as well as the influence of the houseful of women that they live in. Woman, then, is the Captain's nemesis, as it is for many of Strindberg's males. The question is, for all the dynamics of their epic struggle, how does the Captain fight what he knows to be an inevitably unsuccessful battle? One possible and compelling answer is that he doesn't fight, not really, that he chooses not to, that he expects to lose in this battle with his wife over Bertha.

As the play reveals, Laura has been actively against him from the start. In her conversation with her brother the Pastor, we learn that she did not marry the Captain for love, but for security. Adolf was an officer in the cavalry (a socially prestigious position), he was educated, intellectually astute, a freethinker, even a scientist with impressive research papers to his credit: He was a good catch for her purposes.

Strindberg, who was born in the age of Darwin, accepted the proposition of the struggle for survival and the survival of the fittest. And in Strindberg's lexicon, the fittest is the female, who will always have her way, will always win against all odds, including the male's greater physical strength, his schooled intelligence (largely denied women of the time), and his pride of place in a world that denigrated and discounted women.

If this is the case, then Strindberg's Captain must have a very serious flaw that incapacitates him from fighting for his survival. That flaw, as Strindberg makes clear in *The Father,* is the need for sex. From the beginning of their marriage, the Captain has turned a blinkered, or perhaps even a blind eye to Laura's acts to thwart his traditional male primacy in their relationship, and he has done so for one reason: sex. Its demands must be met at any cost— the classical Greek would have called it *ananke*. In effect, the Captain has allowed himself to be systematically destroyed; he commits passive suicide; he does not allow himself to fight (fight, that is, to win, as opposed to putting up the pretence of a fight, if for no other reason than to say to himself that he did his best, which may, in fact, not be entirely incorrect). The male, then, in Strindberg's eyes, is the prey of the female whose one aim is to gain dominance in order to survive at the highest level within her grasp, a level certainly higher than the one a patriarchal construct permits her.

The other side of the coin, however, is every bit as interesting, perhaps even more so. In regard to the full possession of her child, Laura has used ruthless means in her struggle for supremacy. She has deliberately planted the poisonous seed of doubt in his mind that he is not the child's father. Not only is this a devastating blow to the Captain's pride, it is a "fact" that (in the 1880s) he has no way to disprove, since there is only one person who knows for certain—the mother. The second blow (and perhaps the more debilitating of the two) is that this "fact" denies him his immortality. A freethinker, perhaps even an agnostic, the Captain reveals early in the play, before the paternity complication appears, that immortality to him is to live on in his progeny. That, too, is now denied him. Knowing this, Laura moves in for the kill—no mere phrase here—and leads the Captain step-by-step into insanity and subsequent death by stroke.

Strindberg makes the criminality of Laura's *modus operandi* pristinely clear in the third-act discussion between Laura and her brother who unequivocally accuses her of what he has systematically observed, her "little innocent murder." He says to her after asking to see her hands: "Not a single spot of blood to betray you, no hidden trace of poison. A little innocent murder that the law can't get at; an unconscious crime. Unconscious? Remarkable invention!" Every bit as remarkable as the Captain's twenty-year ability to be unconscious of his subservience to Laura in return for the desired reward.

In a letter dated October 17, 1887, the year of the play's composition, Strindberg, recognizing the larger-than-life-size characters of his two principals, wondered who would ultimately play the Captain and Laura. He knew that the play could easily be destroyed by a miscast actor, even made to seem "ridiculous." His advice was to cast an actor "with a generally healthy temperament." Ideally he should possess the "superior, self-ironic, lightly skeptical tone of a man of the world," a man who "conscious of his advantage, goes to meet his fate in a relatively carefree mood, wrapping himself in death in the spider's web he cannot tear to shreds because of natural laws...No screaming, no sermons.—Let's remember that a cavalry officer is always a rich man's son, who has been brought up well, makes high demands on himself in his relations with others and is refined even in dealing with the soldier [Nöjd]. So no crude fool of the traditional variety...Besides, he has risen above his work, has exposed it, and is a scientist. To me he represents especially here a manliness people have tried to disparage, taken away from us, and awarded to the third sex! It is only in the presence of woman he is unmanly, and that is how she wants him, and the law of accommodation forces us to play the role our mistress requires. Yes, we sometimes have to play chaste, ingenuous, ignorant just to get the sexual intercourse we want!"

As for Laura, she should not be played as a virago—that way lies melodrama, as it also does if the Captain is misinterpreted—but as a woman of her time, who, like many of Ibsen's women, is determined to get the upper hand in a male world. She is a product of her society of the mid-19th century who has decided that enough is enough, and who has, perhaps, lost sight of just whom she has married. Neither side is free of blame.

MISS JULIE

With a mind as diverse and conflicted as Strindberg's it should not be surprising that his points of view on even serious matters should change from play to play. If in *The Father* it appears that the female is the victor in the process of evolution, in *Miss Julie,* written within the next year, it is Jean, the servant struggling to rise, who seems to be the winner in the battle for dominance. In a way, it is consistent with another of Strindberg's social perceptions, that the aristocratic class is a degenerate brood of hangers-on. In regard to Jean he wrote, "the son of the people has conquered the white skin." Having himself come from a less than affluent family, he, too, like Jean, had to struggle for position. Jean to him was, as one critic has put it, "the coming gentleman by virtue of his energy and ability"; and yet, he is not a particularly attractive character from the standpoint of who he is, even though Strindberg undoubtedly saw himself in Jean.

Strindberg called *Miss Julie* the first naturalistic play in Scandinavia. And yet it falls short of the full thrust of the naturalist program in its happy failure to regard one of the movement's central tenets, namely the "slice of life" approach to art. Naturalist theater and literature was to eschew the ordering process that had typified art in the past. Life is chaos, insisted the naturalists, and therefore the chaos of life must be at the center of art. Art and life must be, they maintained, synonymous. Art, in the scientific age, must be as objective as a scientific experiment; it must grow out of a scientific study of a small section of life itself (like the study of a culture on the slide of a microscope). Selection and arrangement, to the naturalist, was anathema. Needless to say, the whole movement was a revolt to sweep clean the slate of the excesses of romanticism.

There can be no question that Strindberg, in writing *Miss Julie,* had read and digested his Zola. But he was too much the artist to throw aesthetic selection and order out with the dishwater. In his preface to *Miss Julie,* he acknowledges each of these laws of naturalism, but in actuality he did not swallow them whole. He selected, he chose, he arranged, he ordered, and as a result achieved one of the most durable and brilliantly constructed pieces of theater in the whole range of dramatic composition. Walter Johnson has summed it up as well as anyone.

> Strindberg did consider [*Miss*] *Julie* naturalistic, and, granting the qualifications of selection and arrangement, one will have to admit that Strindberg within those limits has given us an artist's presentation of an inner recreation of a segment of life The one-act form; a theme that is universal and timeless; a plot that was partly taken right out of life and could have been almost completely; a dialogue that strikes one as natural conversation, in terms of the situation, the particular people, the time, and the place; the decidedly realistic setting and staging; and the characterization—all these are in keeping with what Strindberg believed was naturalistic, always, it must be remembered, as seen and heard through Strindberg's eyes and ears and transformed in the creative process.

Having called himself in the title of one of his novels the "son of a servant," Strindberg had his eyes constantly focused on the issue of the upward mobility of the lower classes, and for good reason. He lived at a time in 19th century Sweden when the aristocracy was steadily loosing ground. The 1860s, for example, saw the elimination of the system of the four estates in the Swedish parliament when the House of Lords was abolished (it took England another century and a half just to deal with the issue), an act that promised eventual control by the slowly rising lower classes.

In *Miss Julie* we have the meeting of both ends of the social spectrum, an aristocratic young woman of twenty-five, and the healthy, ruggedly handsome, sexually provocative and ambitious young servant five years her senior. It is Midsummer Eve, June 24, just past the summer solstice when in the northern regions of the globe the day's end seems never to arrive, the body and mind tire but cannot rest, so powerful is the influence of the sun's energy: The effect of the day on the play's events cannot be discounted by anyone who has experienced the phenomenon. Life is a constant buzz, ears ring, blood surges, the mind is not in control—all of which is happily exacerbated by the feast day celebration of St. John the Baptist.

The specific time of the play is only one of the many factors used by

Strindberg to lead to the final tragedy, another being that Miss Julie is having her period. Equally contributory are the recent breakup of her engagement to a young lawyer, Miss Julie's heredity—her mother's lower-class origins, and her radically feminist attitudes, raising her daughter to despise the male sex and to exalt herself as the male's superior, and her father's influence in teaching her to despise her own sex.

One of the most theatrical and informative devises in a Strindberg play is that of parallel action, and *Miss Julie* has two that are of particular brilliance. The first appears early on. Diana, Miss Julie's female dog, has recently escaped its closely protected environment and run off with the gamekeeper's mongrel mutt. Diana is predictably "in trouble," a situation which, we learn, Miss Julie does not want to deal with, therefore she has the cook prepare a concoction to abort the pregnancy, a measure that will most likely kill Diana (though we are not told) and that foreshadows Miss Julie's own attitude regarding her own feared pregnancy. The situation clearly introduces a sharp parallel to Miss Julie's own life. The dog is named Diana after the Roman goddess of chastity and the hunt. There can be no doubt whatever that at the play's beginning Miss Julie is indeed intact, as her constrained and restrictive upbringing has insisted. Diana as goddess of the hunt parallels both the dog's and Miss Julie's breaking loose in pursuit of any avenue of sexual release—both below their station.

Diana is also, we can only assume, a dog of station, an aristocrat of a dog with a pedigree, a pure-breed never meant to mix with the riffraff likes of the gamekeeper's mutt, and carefully protected from doing so. The same must be said of Miss Julie; but Diana does escape, and with a specimen far her inferior, indulging her natural appetite for the first time, just as Miss Julie will do with her servant Jean in the course of the play. At first Miss Julie insisted that Diana be shot for her shameless indiscretion, but she finally decides on an attempt to abort. Miss Julie's solution for herself will be more severe.

Then there is the issue of Serena, Miss Julie's female finch. The tiny bird is pampered, held captive in a cage, and is expected to sing for her captor. Miss Julie, too, is a captive, not in a cage, but in a class and a tradition no less restrictive. One critic has noted the finch's name, Serena, and suggests that "her very name [implies] the serenity of the artificially protected captive to sing appropriately for the pleasure of her human keepers." Just as the finch has its head cut off on the chopping block by a meat clever wielded by Jean, Miss Julie will slice her own throat with the razor that Jean will put in her hand. Possibly the finch's blood spilled by the brutal Jean is, in addition to foreshadowing Miss Julie's eventual suicide, also the sexual blood not only of menstruation (as has been noted by others), but the blood of her first sexual experience at the hands of a human mutt.

Miss Julie's suicide at the play's end is motivated by many things, but one in particular stands out. Like her protected, aristocratic Diana, Miss Julie has fallen from her height and everybody knows it, in particular the servant revelers who enter the empty kitchen and sing a lascivious song while she and Jean are at it in his room. There is no place she can hide and no way she can reassert her former status. Scandal is her nemesis just as surely as it is the nemesis of Hedda Gabler. Hedda is unquestionably pregnant and hates herself for that weakness because it identifies her as female, a fact of herself that she, too, was taught to despise by her father, General Gabler, who raised her as a boy. Miss Julie is most likely pregnant and fears it for herself, as she feared it for Diana, for precisely the same reason as Hedda.

To sum it up, Miss Julie has violated everything she was made to be. She has betrayed her mother's feminism and her father's patriarchalism, the two self-contradictory realities of her being. She is nothing less than no one. In her great, passionate confession to Jean toward the play's conclusion, she finally is able to say: "I don't even have a *self* I can call my own." The two warring sides of her imposed nature cancel each other out and leave her nothing less than nothing.

THE STRONGER

A one-act play—a sketch, really, since it occupies only half a dozen pages at best—written by Strindberg in 1888–89 for his proposed Experimental Theater repertory, was intended for his first wife Siri von Essen in the role of Mrs. X. It is a triangular situation in which two actresses—one married, Mrs. X, and one unmarried, Miss Y—meet accidentally at a café and begin considering their past rivalry in love for Mrs. X's husband. It is unique that the subject of the discussion, the husband, never appears, and for the fact that only one of the women, Mrs. X, speaks, while the other, Miss Y, merely reacts. To say "merely" is, however, to minimize unjustly the silent role, for it presents challenges every bit as great as those offered to Mrs. X.

In *The Stronger* Strindberg demonstrates what a keen insight and capacity for observation he possessed in regard to human nature and its machinations. There is, of course, the fairly open question of which of the two women is the stronger, the married actress who takes all in stride, bends with the winds, and survives in the dog-eat-dog world, or the silent Miss Y who, as

Mrs. X says, has failed to bend and broken like a dry reed. But is her observation correct or is it wishful thinking, for near the end she observes that Miss Y, rather than going after her prey aggressively, merely sits like a cat at the rat hole and outwaits it. Mrs. X may in fact be announcing her own eventual loss of her husband to Miss Y—except that she is currently so secure in her marriage and family that she is unaware of her unconscious premonition. Like all great works, *The Stronger* has built-in ambiguities.

When Siri von Essen asked Strindberg how to play the role of Mrs. X, he replied, in effect, play it: (1) never forgetting that she is an actress—not an ordinary respectable housewife with a family; (2) as the stronger, the more pliant of the two, who bends under pressure, then rises once more; (3) dressed in the height of fashion; (4) if you buy a new coat avoid smooth surfaces and smooth pleats, and buy a new hat, something with fur, bonnet-shaped, and not in the English style; (5) study the role with exacting care, but play it simply, which is to say not too simply, be fifty percent charlatan, and suggest profundities that don't exist.

A DREAM PLAY

The Author's Note to *A Dream Play* states as well as possible the goals of the play that Strindberg called "My most blessed drama, the child of my greatest suffering," and there is no possibility of overstating its importance in the history of western theater. It freed the stage from its naturalistic shackles; it allowed the imagination to soar free of time and space; it permitted a character to split into as many manifestations as it possessed; and it put an end to, dissolved, the concept of total, unified character. The influence of *A Dream Play* has been enormous from the time of its creation, through expressionism, surrealism, and the so-called theater of the absurd down to the present, and it is only in the last few decades that the theater has achieved a plasticity sufficient to do it justice in visual terms.

Between 1898 and 1903 Strindberg experienced his most creative period, during which he wrote in excess of a score of plays, including some of his greatest. His mind was in turmoil both personally and creatively. He was suffering his third and most volatile marriage and perhaps needed to find a new form of theater capable of encompassing the magnitude of his despair which so often became the subject, at least in essence, of his work. As far as the need for a new form of theater—of art in general—is concerned, he was not alone. The foment of a new world was all around him at the century's turn. In 1897 Gustav Klimt founded the Secessionist group of artists—

painters, musicians, sculptors—in Vienna, a breakaway group determined to represent reality not in terms of traditional photographic realism, but to see and convey it in exciting, unexpected, and decorative ways—to get to the bottom of things rather than to be stuck to the surface. The Cubists and abstract painters overthrew the maxim that art consisted in a recognizable object situated in a setting of some sort, whether temporal or spatial. In 1896 Chekhov in *The Seagull* has his Treplev, an unpublished and unperformed young playwright, denounce the traditional theater and cry out for "new forms." This was the rumble that shook the art world at the century's end, and Strindberg was a part of it whether or not he was fully conscious of the fact. Walter Johnson sums up the work with great insight:

> *A Dream Play* presents a remarkably rich and impressively complete treatment of the human condition poetically perceived and poetically presented. It gives us Strindberg's fullest post-Inferno statement of personal belief about the forces controlling the world in which we live, the very texture of that world, and the misery and the glory of human life. It is a statement that is both negative and positive. Strindberg neglects neither the beauty nor the ugliness in the world or in man; he is as aware of the moments of intense joy as he is of the periods of despair and suffering and the boredom of monotonous repetition. The substance of *A Dream Play* may well be said, however, to be an expression of modern pessimism, emphasizing as it does the extreme limitations placed on every human being by his senses and all of his other powers, the extreme difficulty of controlling everyman's key problem—his ego, and the slight possibilities for improvement in a human community made up of individuals, all of whom are struggling not only for survival but for personal advantage and advancement. It is in such matters that what Strindberg says in *A Dream Play*...has interesting parallels with Freud's Adjustment, Adler's Compensation, and Jung's Persona.

THE GHOST SONATA

The principal theme of *The Ghost Sonata* is the discrepancy between appearance and reality, a theme which occupied the minds of many playwrights at the turn of the century, most notably the Viennese Arthur Schnitzler, and the Sicilian Luigi Pirandello.

Michael Meyer, Strindberg's preeminent modern biographer, quotes Strindberg in 1905 as writing: "Life is so horribly ugly, we human beings so utterly evil, that if a writer were to portray everything he saw and heard no one could bear to read it. There are things which I remember having seen and heard in good, respectable and well-liked people, but which I have blotted out from my mind because I could not bring myself to speak of them and do not wish to remember them. Breeding and education are only masks to hide our bestiality and virtue is a sham. The best we can hope for is to conceal our wretchedness. Life is so cynical that only a swine can be happy in it; and any man who sees beauty in life's ugliness is a swine! Life is a punishment. A hell. For some a purgatory, for none a paradise. We are compelled to commit evil and to torment our fellow mortals." It is a statement written midway between *A Dream Play* and *The Ghost Sonata* and in a very profound way unites them thematically.

One cannot watch a performance of *The Ghost Sonata* without shifting in one's seat in discomfort over the bleakness and cruelty of the action on stage. In a letter to his German translator, Strindberg wrote concerning the play, that it is as horrible as life itself when we tear away the veils from our eyes and face reality *per se*. He saw the corruption of life presented in *The Ghost Sonata* as symptomatic of life in general, except that we are too proud to admit it.

Strindberg's characters in the play are based on real people he saw, sometimes daily, on his walks in the upscale Stockholm suburb of Östermalm. The opening scene might serve as a recapitulation of those walks and sights seen, from a young man observed through a window, as Meyer describes it, "playing cards with three old people who looked like mummies," to "a rich old man in a wheel-chair." And Walter Johnson writes that many of Strindberg's plays originated in homes of his own, whereas *The Ghost Sonata* emerged from what he had heard and observed, "and what he had guessed at about the homes of his neighbors."

The themes of *The Ghost Sonata* are two: the idealism represented throughout by the young student Arkenholz, and the vampirism of Hummel, the man in the wheelchair.

There is some evil force in every life, Strindberg maintains, that eats at the very core of our being, that sucks our energy, and destroys our will—and will is a major element in *The Ghost Sonata*, for it is the *raison d'etre* of Hummel, and from the opening tableau of the play it is his power of will that gives him possession if the idealistic young Arkenholz. Will is here as powerful and evil a force as it was in *The Father* and as it appeared in *Miss Julie*, at the end of which the heroine has totally lost her own will and begs Jean to give his to her so that she can use it to carry out her suicide.

In the most profound of ways *The Ghost Sonata* is as poetically conceived as it is possible for a dramatic work to be. In the first place, it is a dream play, a form which allows Strindberg to strip away the defenses we generally use to protect ourselves, the masks, the personas that we assume to make life appear an easier and less deadly burden. Strindberg's plays are frequently close readings, direct analyses of life and people; *The Ghost Sonata* operates on another plane. The place of analysis is taken over by intuition, the reasoning factor is usurped by insight, knowledge comes apocalyptically, as revelation, in a burst of light.

Like *A Dream Play, The Ghost Sonata* is a play of despair over the misery of the human condition. The idealist Arkenholz in the play's final sentences apostrophizes in the dead Daughter the whole of humanity and the impossibility of human compassion. "Poor, dear child, child of this world of delusion, of guilt, suffering, and of death; this world of eternal change, of disappointment, and of pain! May the Lord of Heaven be merciful to you on your journey."

Strindberg's life was one of the most tormented and conflicted of modern times, but out of the dark vision that obsessed him arose some of the most coruscating and exciting theater in the history of world drama.

CARL R. MUELLER
Department of Theater
School of Theater, Film, and Television
University of California, Los Angeles

THE FATHER

A Tragedy in Three Acts

1887

The Father

ACT ONE

Living room of the Captain's house. A door to the right in the rear wall lead-
ing to the entrance hall. Center stage a large round table with newspapers
and magazines. To the right a leather couch with a small table in front of it.
In the right corner a wallpapered door. Left, a desk with a clock, and a door
leading to the inner rooms. Weapons decorate the walls: guns and game bags.
A clothes-tree stands near the rear door on which hang military coats. There
is a lighted lamp on the large table. The CAPTAIN and the PASTOR sit on
the leather couch. The CAPTAIN is in undress uniform with riding boots
and spurs. The PASTOR is in black with a white neck cloth, but without a
clerical collar. He smokes a pipe. The CAPTAIN rings. The ORDERLY enters.

ORDERLY: Sir?

CAPTAIN: Is Nöjd out there?

ORDERLY: In the kitchen, sir, awaiting orders.

CAPTAIN: Oh, not in the kitchen again! Get him in here at once!

ORDERLY: Yes, sir. *(Goes out.)*

PASTOR: *Now* what's the trouble?

CAPTAIN: Been at it with the serving girl again! Got her pregnant! Damn
him!

PASTOR: Nöjd? Same as last year?

CAPTAIN: What else! Have a word with him, won't you? Something
friendly. Maybe it'll take this time. I've about run the gamut. Sworn at
him, thrashed him—he couldn't care less!

PASTOR: I see. Read him a sermon. Hm. May I ask what effect the word of
God will have on a cavalryman?

CAPTAIN: Yes, well, as my brother-in-law you know the effect it's had on me.

PASTOR: Only too well.

CAPTAIN: Well, it might on him. At least give it a try. *(NÖJD enters.)* So,
what have you been up to now, Nöjd, my man?

NÖJD: Excuse me, Captain, sir, I really shouldn't say, what with the Pastor here.

PASTOR: No need to be embarrassed, my boy.

CAPTAIN: All right, let's have it, the whole story—or you know what to expect.

NÖJD: Well, sir, you see, well—I mean, we were dancing up at Gabriel's— and then, well, Ludwig said—

CAPTAIN: Ah! Ludwig! The facts, man, the facts!

NÖJD: Well, sir—I mean, well, then Emma got it in her head to—to go down to the barn and—

CAPTAIN: Aha! So then it was Emma who seduced you!

NÖJD: Well, you're not too far off the mark there, sir, if you know what I mean. If a girl doesn't want to, you can just kiss the whole thing off—if you know what I—

CAPTAIN: I know exactly what you mean! Are you the child's father or aren't you?

NÖJD: Well, sir, how do you know a thing like that, sir?

CAPTAIN: How do you—? What do you mean, how do you know a thing like that!

NÖJD: Well, I mean, that's something you can never be sure of, sir.

CAPTAIN: You weren't the only one, then?

NÖJD: Well, that time, sure, sir, but that's no proof that other times—

CAPTAIN: Ah, so you're blaming Ludwig now, is that it?

NÖJD: It's hard to know exactly who to blame, sir.

CAPTAIN: Then why did you tell Emma you wanted to marry her?

NÖJD: Well, sir, I mean—I mean, it's just—what you say—

CAPTAIN: *(To the PASTOR.)* I can't believe this!

PASTOR: The same old story! But, Nöjd, listen to me—you have to be man enough to know if you're the father.

NÖJD: Well, I mean—well, we did it—sure—you know—but that doesn't mean anything has to come of it.

PASTOR: Listen to me now, young man, this is you we're talking about here! Surely you're not going to abandon that girl with a child to take care of! I dare say we can't force you to marry her, but I assure you, you *will* pay for the child's upkeep! That I promise you!

NÖJD: Maybe so, but Ludwig pays his share, too.

CAPTAIN: Well, then, it goes to court! Let them settle it! This has nothing to do with me, and I couldn't care less! Now get out of here!

PASTOR: Nöjd! One more thing! Hm! Doesn't it disturb you leaving the girl in the lurch like that with a child to take care of? Doesn't it? Have you no sense of honor? Doesn't such behavior strike you as—as—well—?

NÖJD: If I really knew I was the father, then, sure, but I don't know that, no one can. I mean, slaving away for somebody else's kid, I'm not made for that—not me, no, sir! I mean, you and the Captain, sir, can understand that, I know.

CAPTAIN: Get out!

NÖJD: Sir! *(Goes out.)*

CAPTAIN: And stay out of the kitchen, you hear?—*(To the PASTOR.)* Fine scourge of God, *you* are!

PASTOR: What? I thought I laid into him with real gusto.

CAPTAIN: Laid into him! You sat there muttering to yourself!

PASTOR: To be honest about it, I really don't know what to say. There's no question I pity the girl, but I pity the boy, too. And what if he isn't the father? The girl can nurse the child for four months at the orphanage, and then the child is permanently taken care of. Can the boy do as much? Is he a wet nurse? Afterwards she'll find a good position with a respectable family, but the boy's future is as good as washed up if he's discharged from the regiment.

CAPTAIN: One thing's for certain, I wouldn't want to judge the case. The boy isn't exactly innocent, I suppose; it's not something we can prove. But the girl's guilt can't be doubted—if in fact it's guilt we're looking for.

PASTOR: Yes, well, I don't presume to judge anyone. But what were we talking about when this messy little story interrupted us? Ah! Bertha and her confirmation! That was it!

CAPTAIN: Actually it was less about her confirmation than about her whole upbringing. This house is filled with women, everyone of whom wants to bring up my little girl. My mother-in-law wants to turn her into a spiritualist; Laura insists she become an artist; the governess is determined to make a Methodist of her; old Margret, a Baptist; and the kitchen help already have her marching to the Salvation Army drum. Who ever patched a soul together like that! The trouble is that I, who am solely responsible for her education, am thwarted no matter what I do. I have to get her out of this house.

PASTOR: The trouble is you have too many women running this house.

CAPTAIN: You can say that again! It's a cage of tigers! If I don't hold red-hot irons under their noses, they tear me to bits on the spot! Sure, go on, laugh, you bastard! It wasn't enough I married your sister, you had to foist your old stepmother off on me, too!

PASTOR: Well, for God's sake, man, one can't go around living with one's stepmother.

CAPTAIN: No, but mothers-in-law are just fine—as long as they live in other people's houses.

PASTOR: Yes, well, we all have our burdens to bear.

CAPTAIN: Maybe so. Just why does mine have to weigh a ton? I still have my old childhood nurse with me, who thinks I still ought to be wearing bibs. God knows, she's kindness itself, but she just doesn't belong here.

PASTOR: You need to use a firm hand with women, Adolf, but you let them rule you.

CAPTAIN: And I suppose you're going to instruct me how to do that?

PASTOR: Admittedly, my sister Laura was always a bit—difficult, shall we say?

CAPTAIN: Laura may have her moods, but she's not that much of a problem.

PASTOR: Come now, Adolf, let it go—I know how she can be.

CAPTAIN: She was brought up with a lot of romantic notions, and now she's having trouble adjusting to—circumstances. But, after all, she *is* my wife—

PASTOR: And because she's your wife, she's above reproach. No, no, Adolf, you can't fool me. She's the *real* thorn in your side.

CAPTAIN: Whatever! In any case, the house is in an uproar. Laura refuses to let Bertha leave her, and I refuse to let her stay in this bedlam!

PASTOR: Aha, so Laura won't. Well, then, I'm afraid you're in for some heavy weather, my friend. When she was a child, she'd play dead till she got her way, and when she had what she wanted, she'd give it back, saying it wasn't what she wanted, at all, and that all she wanted was to get her way.

CAPTAIN: Really! Even then! Hm! She sometimes works herself into such a state that she frightens me and I think she's ill.

PASTOR: What is it you want for Bertha that you can't agree on? Can't you compromise?

CAPTAIN: You mustn't think I want to turn her into a child prodigy or some kind of image of myself. Nor do I want to play my daughter's pimp and raise her only for marriage. If I do and she doesn't marry, she'd end up a miserable old maid. On the other hand, I refuse to push her into a masculine career requiring years of training, for that would be nothing but a waste if she did marry.

PASTOR: Then what do you want?

CAPTAIN: I want her to become a teacher. If she doesn't marry, she will at least be able to support herself and be no worse off that those poor male teachers who have to share their salaries with their families. If she *does* marry, she can use what she knows to educate her children. Am I right, or not?

PASTOR: Yes, of course, perfectly. But, on the other hand, what about her talent for painting? Hasn't she shown that? To suppress it would be a crime against nature.

CAPTAIN: No! I showed some of her work to a very well-known painter, and he said it's no better than the kind of thing they learn in school. But then last summer some young know-it-all comes along who has a far better grasp of the situation and declares she has a colossal talent, and that was all Laura needed to set her off.

PASTOR: Was he in love with the girl?

CAPTAIN: I take that entirely for granted!

PASTOR: In which case, I wish you God's help, old boy, because His help is precisely what you'll need. This isn't going to be easy; and, of course, Laura has her own rooting section—in there.

CAPTAIN: You can count on it! This whole house is ready to explode. And just between us, it's not exactly a noble fight they're fighting.

PASTOR: *(Gets up.)* Do you think I don't know?

CAPTAIN: So you know, then?

PASTOR: Who better?

CAPTAIN: The worst of it all, as I see it, is that Bertha's future is being decided in there out of the most despicable of motives—sheer hatred. They drop hints about men having to learn the power of women. It's man against woman in there, without stop.—No, now, you don't have to go, do you? Stay for supper. Nothing special, really, but all the same. I'm expecting the new doctor. But you know that. Have you seen him?

PASTOR: I caught a glimpse of him driving past. He appears to be a pleasant, trustworthy sort.

CAPTAIN: I see. Good. Do you think he might take my side in this?

PASTOR: Who knows? It depends on how much experience he has with women.

CAPTAIN: Oh, come on now, won't you stay?

PASTOR: Thank you, no. I promised I'd be home for dinner. My wife gets very uneasy when I'm late.

CAPTAIN: Uneasy? Angry is more like it. Well, whatever. Let me help you with your coat.

PASTOR: Must be awfully cold tonight. Thanks. And take care of yourself, Adolf, your health, I mean. You're looking terribly nervous.

CAPTAIN: Nervous, do I ?

PASTOR: Yes, aren't you feeling well?

CAPTAIN: I suppose Laura's put that into your head? For twenty years she's treated me as if I had one foot in the grave.

PASTOR: Laura? No, but I am uneasy about you. Take care of yourself. That's my advice. Good-bye. Oh, but wait, didn't you want to discuss Bertha's confirmation?

CAPTAIN: No, what's the use? Why interfere with the public conscience? Better to let it just take its course. I'm not cut out to be a martyr. For truth? Forget it. We're beyond all that. Good-bye. Remember me to your wife.

PASTOR: Good-bye, Adolf. My love to Laura.

CAPTAIN: *(Opens the desk and sits down to work on accounts.)* Thirty-four—nine, forty-three—seven, eight, fifty-six.

LAURA: *(Enters from another part of the house.)* Would you be so kind as to—

CAPTAIN: One moment!—Sixty-six, seventy-one, eighty-four, eighty-nine, ninety-two, one hundred. What is it?

LAURA: Perhaps I'm disturbing you.

CAPTAIN: Not at all. The household money, I suppose?

LAURA: Yes, the household money.

CAPTAIN: Put the accounts down there, then I'll go through them.

LAURA: The accounts?

CAPTAIN: Yes.

LAURA: I'm to keep accounts now?

CAPTAIN: Accounts? Of course. Our financial situation is precarious at the moment, and in the event of an audit I'd have to produce records or be charged with negligence.

LAURA: The state of our finances is not my fault.

CAPTAIN: That's precisely what the accounts will prove.

LAURA: Our tenant farmer not paying his rent is not my fault.

CAPTAIN: And who was it recommended this tenant farmer so enthusiastically? You! Why did you do that? Why did you recommend such a—such—careless fool?

LAURA: Why did you take on such a careless fool?

CAPTAIN: Because I wasn't allowed to eat in peace, to sleep in peace, to work in peace, until you got him here. You wanted him because your brother wanted to be rid of him; your mother wanted him because I didn't want him; the governess wanted him because he was a pietist; and old Margret because she'd known his grandmother since they were children together. That's why I took him on, and if I hadn't, I'd be a raving lunatic in a madhouse now or lying six feet under in the family plot. In any case, here's your household money and your allowance. You can give me your accounts later.

LAURA: *(Curtsies.)* Thank you so much! And you, do you keep accounts of personal expenses?

CAPTAIN: That's none of your business.

LAURA: That's true, yes, as little as my child's upbringing is none of my business. Did you gentlemen reach a decision after your evening session?

CAPTAIN: My decision had already been reached, and therefore I had only to report it to the one friend I and this family have in common. Bertha will be boarding in town and will be leaving two weeks from today.

LAURA: Boarding with whom, if I may ask?

CAPTAIN: With the Sävbergs.

LAURA: That freethinker!

CAPTAIN: According to the law, a child is to be brought up in its father's faith.

LAURA: And the mother has nothing to say about it?

CAPTAIN: Nothing. She sold her birthright in a binding legal agreement, and relinquished her rights in exchange for the husband's support of her and her children.

LAURA: So the mother has no rights over her child?

CAPTAIN: None whatever. You don't sell something, then take it back and keep the money.

LAURA: But if the father and mother would both agree—

CAPTAIN: How could we? I want her to live in town, you want her to live out here. The compromise would be that she live at the railroad station midway between town and home. This is a problem with no resolution. Do you see?

LAURA: Then we must resolve it with force.—What was Nöjd doing here earlier?

CAPTAIN: That's a professional secret.

LAURA: Which the whole kitchen knows.

CAPTAIN: Splendid! Then you must know all about it!

LAURA: Oh, I do.

CAPTAIN: And, no doubt, have already handed down your verdict.

LAURA: The law lays it out quite clearly.

CAPTAIN: What the law doesn't lay out is who is the child's father.

LAURA: One usually knows.

CAPTAIN: Wise men say one can never tell such things.

LAURA: How remarkable! Not know the father of a child?

CAPTAIN: It's what they say!

LAURA: Remarkable! Then how does the father have such rights over her child?

CAPTAIN: He has such rights after he has assumed certain responsibilities, or has had those responsibilities forced upon him. And in marriage, of course, there can be no doubt about paternity.

LAURA: No doubt?

CAPTAIN: I should certainly hope not.

LAURA: Not even if the wife has been unfaithful?

CAPTAIN: That has no bearing on the present discussion. Anything else you're curious about?

LAURA: Nothing.

CAPTAIN: Then I'm going to my room, and be so good as to inform me when the doctor arrives. *(Closes the desk and gets up.)*

LAURA: Of course.

CAPTAIN: *(Going out through the wallpapered door at the right.)* The minute he arrives. I don't want to seem impolite. You understand! *(Goes out.)*

LAURA: I understand! *(Looks at the money in her hand.)*

MOTHER-IN-LAW: *(From another room.)* Laura!

LAURA: Yes!

MOTHER-IN-LAW: Where's my tea?

LAURA: *(In the doorway, left.)* I'll bring it in a moment! *(Goes to the entrance door at the rear just as the ORDERLY opens it and appears.)*

ORDERLY: Dr Östermark.

DOCTOR: *(Enters.)* Madam!

(The ORDERLY goes out, closing the door.)

LAURA: *(Goes toward him and extends her hand.)* How do you do, Doctor. How nice to see you. The captain is out just now, but he'll be back shortly.

DOCTOR: I apologize for coming so late, but I've been making house calls.

LAURA: Do sit down.

DOCTOR: Thank you.

LAURA: Yes, there's been considerable illness in the area recently, but I hope you'll find it to your liking all the same. For people as isolated here in the country as we are, it's important to find a doctor who takes his patients seriously. I've heard so many good things about you, Doctor. I trust we'll get along well together.

DOCTOR: You're very kind, but I hope for your sake my visits here won't too often be out of necessity. I understand your family is in quite good health—

LAURA: No serious illnesses, fortunately. Still, not everything is quite as it should be.

DOCTOR: Indeed!

LAURA: No, not at all as we might wish.

DOCTOR: Really! You frighten me.

LAURA: Every family has circumstances that it finds necessary to hide from the general view—

DOCTOR: Except from the doctor.

LAURA: That's why it's my painful duty to tell you everything from the start.

DOCTOR: Perhaps we should postpone this till I've had the honor of meeting your husband.

LAURA: No! You must hear me out first *before* you meet him.

DOCTOR: Then it has to do with him?

LAURA: Yes, him—my poor dear husband.

DOCTOR: You make me uneasy, madam, but I assure you, you have my full sympathy.

LAURA: *(Taking out a handkerchief.)* My husband is mentally ill. There, now, I've said it. You can judge for yourself when you meet him.

DOCTOR: I find this hard to believe! I've read the captain's excellent articles on mineralogy and admired them very much. They exhibit a keen and powerful intellect.

LAURA: Is that so? Yes, well, it would make all of us in this family very happy to have been mistaken.

DOCTOR: He may, of course, be disturbed in other areas. Would you care to tell me about it—

LAURA: That's exactly what has us so frightened! You see, at times he has the strangest ideas—ideas which he's entitled to as a scholar—if only they didn't affect the well-being of his entire family. For example, he has this obsession for buying things.

DOCTOR: That's unfortunate. What does he buy?

LAURA: Books! Whole boxes of them—that he never reads.

DOCTOR: Well, but for a scholar that's hardly a derangement.

LAURA: You don't believe what I'm saying.

DOCTOR: Not at all. I'm convinced you believe what you're saying.

LAURA: But is it possible to look through a microscope and see what's happening on another planet?

DOCTOR: Does he say he can do that?

LAURA: He does, yes.

DOCTOR: Through a microscope?

LAURA: Through a microscope, yes.

DOCTOR: If this is true, then this is indeed serious.

LAURA: If this is true! Then you have no confidence in me, Doctor! And here I am telling you our family secret!

DOCTOR: I have every confidence in you, madam, and it honors me. But I'm a doctor; I have to examine, I have to observe, before I make a judgment. Has the captain ever shown symptoms of capriciousness, of extreme vacillation of will?

LAURA: Has he, you ask? Doctor, we've been married for twenty years and never once has he made up his mind without changing it afterward.

DOCTOR: Is he obstinate?

LAURA: He insists on having his own way, then when he has it, he throws it all overboard and asks me to decide.

DOCTOR: Yes, this is serious. It will require close observation. The backbone of the mind is the will, you see. Injure the will, and the mind goes to pieces.

LAURA: God knows what I've put up with during these long years of trial. Forcing myself to agree with him. You have no idea what I've had to endure. Always by his side.

DOCTOR: Your misfortune touches me deeply. I'll do all I can to see what needs doing. I only ask that you trust me totally. But from what I've just heard, I must warn you of one thing. Avoid any subject with strong emotional associations for your husband. In a sick mind they can spread like wildfire and end up obsessions and manias. Do you understand?

LAURA: In other words, don't make him suspicious.

DOCTOR: Exactly! You can make a sick man believe anything because he's receptive to everything.

LAURA: Yes, of course. I understand. (*A bell rings from inside.*) Excuse me, that's my mother ringing. Could you wait a bit? Ah, but here's Adolf! (*LAURA leaves as the CAPTAIN enters through the wallpapered door at the right.*)

CAPTAIN: Ah, so you've arrived, Doctor? You're very welcome!

DOCTOR: Captain! What a great pleasure to meet so celebrated a scientist!

CAPTAIN: Oh, please, no! My professional obligations leave no time for in-depth research. But I do think I'm on the track of a real discovery!

DOCTOR: Really!

CAPTAIN: Oh, yes! I've been subjecting meteorites to spectroanalysis and discovered carbon, which is to say vestiges of organic life. What do you say to that?

DOCTOR: Can you see that through a microscope?

CAPTAIN: Oh, good heavens, no! Through a spectroscope!

DOCTOR: Ah! A spectroscope! I beg your pardon! In that case, you'll soon be telling us what's happening on Jupiter.

CAPTAIN: Not happening, exactly, but what *has* happened. If only that damned bookseller in Paris would send me the books! Actually I think all the booksellers in the world are conspired against me. In two months I've had not one reply to any of my orders! Not one, to all of my letters and nasty telegrams! It's driving me insane! How can this have happened?

DOCTOR: Carelessness would be my guess. You mustn't get so worked up over it.

CAPTAIN: But, damn it all, I won't be able to finish my paper on time! Besides, they're working along the same lines in Berlin! But this is hardly what we should be talking about. You're the subject! So! Tell me, would you like to live here? If so, we have a small apartment available in the wing. Or perhaps you'd prefer living in the old doctor's official residence.

DOCTOR: Whatever you say.

CAPTAIN: No, whatever *you* say. It's your decision.

DOCTOR: No, it's for you to decide, Captain.

CAPTAIN: I decide absolutely nothing. Say what you want. I have no preference. None.

DOCTOR: I'm afraid I just can't decide—

CAPTAIN: For Christ's sake, man, say what you want! I have no will in this matter, no opinion, no wishes! Are you such a simpleton you don't know what you want? Speak up, before I get angry!

DOCTOR: All right, since it's up to me, I'll live here.

CAPTAIN: Good! Thank you! Ah! Forgive me, Doctor, but nothing infuriates me more than hearing people say they are indifferent to anything. *(He rings. The NURSE enters.)* Ah, so it's you, Margret. Would you know if the apartment in the wing is ready for the doctor?

NURSE: Yes, it is, Captain.

CAPTAIN: So! Then I won't detain you, Doctor. You must be tired. Goodbye, and welcome once again. I'll see you tomorrow, I hope.

DOCTOR: Good evening, Captain!

CAPTAIN: I trust my wife has explained circumstances around here to you, so that you have some idea of the lay of the land.

DOCTOR: She filled me in on a detail or two that she thought a stranger ought to know. Good evening, Captain. *(Goes off.)*

CAPTAIN: *(To the NURSE.)* Tell me now, old dear. Was there something you wanted?

NURSE: You must listen to me, Mr. Adolf—you must.

CAPTAIN: Then you go right ahead, my dear. Speak out. You're the only one I can listen to around here without falling into a rage.

NURSE: All right, then, Mr. Adolf, you just listen. I was thinking, maybe you could meet the mistress halfway in this matter about the child. After all, she's the mother, and—

CAPTAIN: After all, I'm the father, Margret.

NURSE: There, there, now! A father has all sorts of things besides his child, but a mother has only her child.

CAPTAIN: Exactly. She has one burden, I have three, and hers as well. Can you imagine me staying a soldier all my life if I hadn't had her and her child?

NURSE: Yes, but that's not what I meant.

CAPTAIN. No, I'm sure not. You wanted me to be in the wrong.

NURSE: Don't you believe I want the best for you, Mr. Adolf?

CAPTAIN: Yes, you old dear, I do believe it, but you don't *know* what's best for me. It's not enough to have given life to the child; I want to give her my soul, too.

NURSE: Yes, well, I don't know much about such things. I just think you two could try to get along together.

CAPTAIN: Then you're not my friend, after all, Margret!

NURSE: Me? Not your friend? How can you say such a thing, Mr. Adolf? Do you think I can forget that you were my child when your were little?

CAPTAIN: No, my old dear—no more than I can. You've been like a mother to me, supported me when all of them were against me, but now when I need you most, you desert me for the enemy.

NURSE: Enemy!

CAPTAIN: Yes, enemy! You know the ups and downs of everything in this house. You've seen it all, everything, from beginning to end.

NURSE: Yes, and more than I'd like to admit to. But why in God's name do two people torment the life out of each other—two people who in every other way are so good and want to do right by others? The mistress is never like that to me or to anyone else—

CAPTAIN: Only to me. I know. But I'll tell you something, Margret. Desert me and you'll have done a bad thing. They're spinning a web around me to catch me up, and that doctor is not my friend.

NURSE: Oh, but, Mr. Adolf, you think evil of everyone, and it's all to do with faith, you don't have the true one. That's it, that's what it is.

CAPTAIN: And you and the Baptists have found the one, true and only faith. How happy you must be!

NURSE: At least I'm not as unhappy as you, Mr. Adolf. Humble your heart and you'll see the happiness God will give you. You'll love your neighbor.

CAPTAIN: It's amazing. You no sooner begin talking about God and love and your voice becomes hard and your eyes gleam with hatred. No, Margret, there's no way you can have found the true faith.

NURSE: You're very proud and hard in your learning, Mr. Adolf. But when it comes right down to it, it won't amount to much in the end.

CAPTAIN: You and your humble heart speak very arrogantly, I must say. And, yes, I know, learning is of little use to creatures like you.

NURSE: Shame on you! Shame! But all the same, old Margret loves her big, big boy best, and he'll come back to her like a good child when the storm breaks.

CAPTAIN: Margret! I'm sorry—forgive me—but believe me when I say that there's no one here who wishes me well but you. Help me. There's something going to happen I feel it. What, I don't know. But whatever it is, it's evil. *(A scream comes from an inner room.)* What's that? Who's screaming?

BERTHA: *(Runs in from an inner room.)* Papa, papa! Help me! Save me!

CAPTAIN: My dear child, what is it? Tell me!

BERTHA: Help me! I think she's going to hurt me!

CAPTAIN: Who's going to hurt you? Tell me! Tell me!

BERTHA: Grandma! But it's my fault—I tricked her!

CAPTAIN: Go on, go on!

BERTHA: Yes, but please don't say anything! Not to anyone! Promise?

CAPTAIN: Just tell me what it is.

(The NURSE goes out.)

BERTHA: Well—every evening she turns the lamp down low and has me sit at the table with a piece of paper and a pen—and she says the spirits are going to write.

CAPTAIN: What is this nonsense! And you never told me?

BERTHA: I'm sorry—I was afraid—grandma says the spirits get back at a person if they tell. And then the pen starts to write, and I don't know if it's me writing or not. And sometimes it writes a lot, but sometimes not at all. And when I get tired, nothing comes, but she says it has to come, it has to. And tonight I thought it was going so well, but grandma said it was all out of some silly old poem or other, and that I was playing a trick on her, and she got terribly angry.

CAPTAIN: Do you believe in spirits?

BERTHA: I don't know!

CAPTAIN: But I know—and there aren't any!

BERTHA: Grandma says you don't understand such things, and that you have much worse things, things that can see all the way to other planets.

CAPTAIN: She says that? Does she? And what else does she say?

BERTHA: She says that you can't work magic.

CAPTAIN: I never said I could. You know what meteorites are—rocks that have fallen to earth from other heavenly bodies. I can examine such rocks and tell whether they contain the same elements as the earth. That's all I can see.

BERTHA: Grandma says there are things she can see that you can't.

CAPTAIN: Then she's lying.

BERTHA: Grandma doesn't tell lies!

CAPTAIN: Why not?

BERTHA: Then mother tells lies, too!

CAPTAIN: Hm!

BERTHA: And if you say mother lies, I'll never believe you again!

CAPTAIN: I never said that, and that's why you must believe me when I say that for your own good, for your future good, you must leave this house! Would you like that? Would you like to go to town and learn something useful?

BERTHA: Oh, I'd love to, papa! Live in town! Away from here! Anywhere! Just so I get to see you sometime—often. It's so gloomy here, so heavy—like a long winter's night. But when you come, papa, it's like taking out the storm windows on a spring morning and opening up to fresh air!

CAPTAIN: My dear child! My dear-dear child!

BERTHA: But, papa, you have to try to be nice to mother. She cries so often!

CAPTAIN: Hm. So you want to live in town?

BERTHA: Oh, yes!

CAPTAIN: Suppose mother doesn't want that?

BERTHA: But she has to!

CAPTAIN: And if she doesn't?

BERTHA: Then I just don't know what will happen. But she has to, has to!

CAPTAIN: Will you ask her?

BERTHA: No, you ask her, papa. Real nice and sweet. She never listens to me.

CAPTAIN: Hm! Well, now, if you want it, and I want it, and she doesn't want it, where will that put us?

BERTHA: Back in our usual old muddle. Why can't you two—?

LAURA: *(Enters.)* Ah, so here she is! Good! Perhaps now we can hear her opinion on the matter, considering her entire future is about to be decided.

CAPTAIN: What can a young girl know about her future, particularly one with no experience of life. We at least are partially qualified, having seen many a young girl grow up.

LAURA: But since we can't agree, let Bertha decide.

CAPTAIN: No! No one usurps my rights! Neither women nor children! Bertha, leave us!

(BERTHA goes out.)

LAURA: You were afraid to hear what she'd say. Afraid she'd side with me.

CAPTAIN: No, I know what she wants, and I know she wants to get away from home. But I also know that you have the power to change her mind to suit your own purpose.

LAURA: Am I as powerful as all that?

CAPTAIN: Oh, you have a satanic way of getting what you want—but so do most people who don't scruple over what means they use. Dr. Nordling, for example. How did you get rid of him and then connive to bring the new one out here?

LAURA: Yes, how did I manage that?

CAPTAIN: You insulted Nordling until he left, then had your brother scrape up votes to bring the new one out.

LAURA: That was not only easy but entirely legal. Will Bertha be leaving home?

CAPTAIN: Yes, she'll be going two weeks from today.

LAURA: Then that's your decision?

CAPTAIN: Yes.

LAURA: Have you spoken to Bertha about it?

CAPTAIN: Yes.

LAURA: Then I must put a stop to it.

CAPTAIN: You can't.

LAURA: Can't I? What kind of mother allows her daughter to live among people who teach her that everything her mother told her is wrong, and then be despised by her for the rest of her life?

CAPTAIN: What kind of father allows ignorant and conceited women to teach his daughter that her father is a charlatan?

LAURA: It should matter much less to a father.

CAPTAIN: Why?

LAURA: Because a mother is closer to her child, and because it has been discovered that there is no way to know who a child's father is.

CAPTAIN: And that has what to do with us?

LAURA: That you can never know whether you are Bertha's father.

CAPTAIN: Don't I know?

LAURA: No. If there's no way to know, how can you?

CAPTAIN: Is this some kind of joke?

LAURA: No. I'm merely repeating what you taught me. Besides, how can you know that I haven't been unfaithful?

CAPTAIN: I could believe you capable of almost anything, just not that. And if it were true, you'd never admit to it.

LAURA: Let's assume I were prepared to endure anything to keep control over my child—be hated, be shunned, anything. And then let's assume I'm telling the truth now when I say to you that Bertha is *my* child, but not yours. Let's assume—

CAPTAIN: Stop!

LAURA: Assume—just assume. In which case your hold over the child would be ended.

CAPTAIN: Only when you had proved I wasn't her father.

LAURA: That wouldn't be too difficult. Is that what you want?

CAPTAIN: Stop!

LAURA: I'd only need to name the real father, the time, the place. For example—when was Bertha born?—three years after our marriage.

CAPTAIN: Stop this, or—

LAURA: Or what? Yes, I think it is time we stopped. Just be very careful before you make a decision. Most of all, don't make yourself ridiculous.

CAPTAIN: I find this all terribly sad.

LAURA: Which makes you all the more ridiculous.

CAPTAIN: But not you!

LAURA: No. We women have arranged things much too cleverly for you.

CAPTAIN: And that's why you can't be fought with.

LAURA: Then why fight a superior enemy?

CAPTAIN: Superior?

LAURA: Yes. It's odd, but I've never looked at a man without feeling his superior.

CAPTAIN: Well, you're about to meet your superior, and I promise you won't forget it.

LAURA: That will be interesting.

NURSE: *(Enters.)* Dinner's ready. Will you come eat now?

LAURA: Thank you.

(The CAPTAIN hesitates, then sits in an armchair beside the table in front of the couch.)

LAURA: Aren't you coming to eat?

CAPTAIN: Thank you, no, I don't want anything.

LAURA: Depressed?

CAPTAIN: No, simply not hungry.

LAURA: Come along, or they'll be asking questions—unnecessary ones. Be reasonable. No? All right, then, just go on sitting there. *(Goes out.)*

NURSE: Mr. Adolf! What is all this?

CAPTAIN: I don't know what it is. How can a grown man be treated as if he were a child? Can you explain that?

NURSE: Not really. Except that all men, boys or grown-ups, are born of woman—

CAPTAIN: But no woman is born of man. I *am* Bertha's father, Margret! I am! You believe me, don't you? Don't you?

NURSE: Goodness, how childish you are! Of course you're your own child's father. Now come and eat, and don't sit there brooding. There, there, now, come on!

CAPTAIN: Get out, woman! To hell with all you witches! *(Goes to the hall door.)* Svärd, Svärd!

ORDERLY: *(Enters.)* Sir!

CAPTAIN: Hitch up the sleigh! At once!

(The ORDERLY goes out.)

NURSE: Captain, no, listen!

CAPTAIN: Get out, woman! Now!

NURSE: Lord preserve us, what's to come of all this?

CAPTAIN: *(Puts on his cap and prepares to go out.)* Don't expect me! Before midnight! *(Goes off.)*

NURSE: Sweet Jesus, how will all this end?

END OF ACT I

ACT TWO

The lamp on the table is burning. Night. DR. ÖSTERMARK and LAURA are in conversation.

DOCTOR: Judging by my conversation with him, I'm not at all convinced that the evidence bears out your fears. In the first place, you were mistaken in saying he'd arrived at his planetary conclusions by means of a microscope. Now that I know it to be a spectroscope, it frees him from all suspicion of mental derangement. He has, in fact, performed a scientific experiment of the highest order.

LAURA: Yes, but I never said that.

DOCTOR: Madam, I took careful notes of our conversation, precisely on that point, because I thought I had misheard you. One can't be too cautious in making accusations that may lead to a man's being certified.

LAURA: Certified?

DOCTOR: Surely you know that the insane lose all civil and family rights.

LAURA: No, I didn't know that.

DOCTOR: Yes, and there was another point that struck me as questionable. He mentioned that his letter to booksellers had gone unanswered. You'll pardon me for asking, but is it possible you intercepted those letters? Out of purely well-intentioned motives, of course.

LAURA: Yes—yes, I did. I had a duty to protect my family. I could hardly let him ruin us all without doing something.

DOCTOR: Excuse me, but did you consider the consequences of such an action? If he discovers your secret meddling in his affairs, his suspicions will grow with the speed of an avalanche. What's more, in fact, you have obstructed his will, and in doing so stirred up his impatience even more. Surely you know from personal experience how frustrating it is to have your strongest wishes thwarted and your will paralyzed.

LAURA: Oh, yes!

DOCTOR: Then judge how he must have felt.

LAURA: *(Getting up.)* It's midnight and he's still not home. We can expect the worst.

DOCTOR: Could you tell me what happened this evening after I left? I need to know.

LAURA: He rambled on in the most extraordinary way. I mean—can you imagine!—he actually doubted whether he was the father of his own child!

DOCTOR: Strange. Very strange, indeed. Where did that come from?

LAURA: I can't imagine. Unless, of course—well, earlier he questioned one of his men in a paternity case, and when I took the girl's side, he became excited and said that it was impossible to know with certainty who was a child's father. God knows I did all I could to calm him, but now I can only think there's no more we can do. *(Cries.)*

DOCTOR: I'm sorry, but this has simply got to stop. Something must be done, without, of course, rousing his suspicions. Tell me, has the Captain suffered such delusions before?

LAURA: Six years ago. The same thing, exactly. In a letter to his doctor he admitted that he feared for his sanity.

DOCTOR: Yes, I see, I see—obviously a problem very deeply rooted. Then, of course, there's the sanctity of family life, and all that. I have no right to pry, and so I must limit myself to what can be observed. Unfortunately, what's done cannot be undone—but a cure should have been started long ago. Where do you think he might be?

LAURA: I have no idea. It's just that he gets these crazy notions.

DOCTOR: Would you like me to wait up for him? To avoid suspicion, I could say I was here tending your mother who isn't feeling well.

LAURA: Thank you, that would be fine. But please don't leave us, Doctor. You have no idea how worried I am! But wouldn't it better to admit to him from the start what you think of his condition?

DOCTOR: That's something we don't do with the mentally ill. Unless, of course, the patient brings it up—but even then, only rarely. It depends on how things develop. But we shouldn't be found here in any case. Do you mind if I move into the next room? It will appear more natural.

LAURA: Yes, that's much better, and then Margret can sit here. She always waits up for him when he's out. She's also the only one who can manage him. *(Goes to the door on the left.)* Margret! Margret!

NURSE: *(Enters.)* Yes, ma'am! Has the master come?

LAURA: No, but I want you to sit here and wait for him. And when he comes, say that my mother took sick and that's why the doctor is here.

NURSE: Yes, ma'am, all right, I'll see to it.

LAURA: *(At the door, left.)* Will you come this way, Doctor?

DOCTOR: Thank you.

(They go off.)

NURSE: *(Sits at the table, picks up a hymnbook and puts on her glasses.)* Yes, yes! Yes, yes! *(Reads half to herself.)*

How wretched, ah, how sad a thing
Is life here in this vale of tears.
Death's angel hovers ever near
And trumps to all the suffering:
    "Vanity is all, is all!"
Yes, yes! Yes, yes!
    All that lives on earth is grass,
    All creatures great and small must fall,
    And only sorrow, of us all,
    Is left to etch on the tomb, alas:
        "Vanity is all, is all!"
Yes, yes!

BERTHA: *(Enters with a tray of coffee and some embroidery work; she speaks softly.)* Margret, may I sit here with you? It's so ghastly up there!

NURSE: Sweet Jesus, are you still up, child?

BERTHA: I have to sew on papa's Christmas present, you see. And, look here, I've brought you something good!

NURSE: But, my dear, sweet child, this won't do! You have to get up in the morning. It's past twelve.

BERTHA: So? I just can't sit up there alone. There are ghosts up there. I know!

NURSE: There now! What did I tell you! You just mark my words! There are no good fairies looking over this house. What did you hear?

BERTHA: I heard someone singing in the attic, is what.

NURSE: In the attic! At this time of night!

BERTHA: Yes, and it was a sad song, so very, very sad, the saddest song I ever heard. It sounded like it came from the attic room—the one where the cradle is stored—to the left.

NURSE: Dear-oh-dear! And a storm blowing up! The chimneys will blow down, I know! *(She reads from the hymnbook.)* "What is life but toil and pain? A ray of hope, then all in vain!" Dear child, pray God will send us a happy Christmas!

BERTHA: Margret? Is it true? Is papa ill?

NURSE: Yes, I'm afraid so.

BERTHA: Then I guess we won't celebrate Christmas. But how can he be up if he's sick?

NURSE: It's a kind of sickness he doesn't have to stay in bed. Shh! There's someone in the hall! Go to bed now and take the coffee things with you. Or he'll be angry.

BERTHA: *(Going out with the tray.)* Good night, Margret!

NURSE: Good night, dear child! God bless you!

CAPTAIN: *(Enters and removes his cap and overcoat.)* Are you still up? Go to bed!

NURSE: I only wanted to wait till—*(The CAPTAIN lights a candle, opens his desk, sits down at it, and takes letters and newspapers out of his pocket.)* Mr. Adolf.

CAPTAIN: What do you want?

NURSE: The old lady is sick. And the doctor's here.

CAPTAIN: Anything serious?

NURSE: No, I don't believe so. Only a cold.

CAPTAIN: *(Gets up.)* Who was the father of your child, Margret?

NURSE: Goodness, I've told you so many times I can't even count! That scalawag Johansson.

CAPTAIN: Are you certain?

NURSE: How childish! Of course I'm certain. There was no one else.

CAPTAIN: Yes, but did *he* know there was no one else? No, there was no way. But *you* knew. That's the difference.

NURSE: Difference? What difference?

CAPTAIN: No, you can't see it, of course, but it's there all the same. *(Leafs through a photograph album on the table.)* Would you say Bertha looks like me? *(Looks at a photograph in the album.)*

NURSE: As like as two peas in a pod.

CAPTAIN: Did Johansson admit to being the father?

NURSE: Did he have a choice?

CAPTAIN: How terrible! There's the doctor! *(The DOCTOR enters.)* Good evening, Doctor! How is my mother-in-law?

DOCTOR: Nothing serious, really. A slight sprain in the left foot.

CAPTAIN: I thought you said it was a cold, Margret. There seem to be conflicting diagnoses of the ailment. Go to bed, Margret. *(The NURSE goes out.)* Do sit down, Doctor.

DOCTOR: *(Sits down.)* Thank you.

CAPTAIN: Is it true that if you cross a zebra with a mare, you get stripped foals?

DOCTOR: *(Astonished.)* Quite right! Yes!

CAPTAIN: And is it true that if you breed those foals with a stallion, the new foals will be stripped?

DOCTOR: Yes, that's also true.

CAPTAIN: Under certain conditions, then, a stallion can be the sire of stripped foals and vice verse?

DOCTOR: It would appear so.

CAPTAIN: Which is to say, the resemblance of the offspring to the father proves nothing.

DOCTOR: I—well—

CAPTAIN: Which is to say, paternity is beyond proof.

DOCTOR: Yes—well—

CAPTAIN: You are a widower with children?

DOCTOR: I—yes—

CAPTAIN: Hasn't it ever struck you how ridiculous you are as a father? Is there anything quite so amusing as a father parading his children down the street, or hearing a father talk about his children? "My wife's children," he should say. Did you never feel the falseness of your position, never any small pangs of doubt—I won't say suspicions, for I assume that as a gentleman your wife was above reproach.

DOCTOR: No, never. But if I may say so, Captain, a man must take his children on trust, as, I think, Goethe says somewhere.

CAPTAIN: On trust? Where a woman's involved? That's risky!

DOCTOR: Ah, but there are so many kinds of women.

CAPTAIN: No! Only one! Modern research has made that clear! When I was young, I was strong and—I don't mind saying—handsome. I remember at the time having two momentary impressions that since then have led me to doubt this. I was traveling once by steamboat and I and a few friends were in the salon. A young waitress came and sat down opposite me, her eyes red from weeping, and told us that her fiancé had been lost at sea, drowned. We offered our sympathies, and I remember ordering champagne. After the second glass, I touched her foot; after the fourth, her knee. Before morning, I had consoled her.

DOCTOR: Even the sun has spots, Captain.

CAPTAIN: As does the leopard. Now for my second example. I was at a resort on the coast. There was a young woman there with her children, while her husband was away in town on business. She was religious, with the strictest of principles, read me lectures on morality—a totally virtuous, honorable woman. I lent her a book, two books, in fact, and when she was preparing to leave, she unexpectedly returned them. Three months later I found a calling card in one of the books that was a fairly clear declaration. It was quite innocent, about as innocent as a declaration of love from a married woman to a man who had made no advances to her can be. Now for the moral of our tale. Never believe anyone too much!

DOCTOR: Nor too little!

CAPTAIN: No, not that either! But you see, Doctor, that woman was so unconsciously evil that she actually confided her infatuation with me to her husband. And that's exactly where the danger lies—the unconsciousness of their instinctive duplicity. Admittedly it's an extenuating circumstance, but it does nothing to cancel out my judgment, only mitigate it.

DOCTOR: Captain, your thoughts are taking an unhealthy turn—you need to control them.

CAPTAIN: Never use the word unhealthy, Doctor! All steam boilers explode when they reach their limit, but the limit is not the same for all steam boilers. Do you understand? In any case, you're here to keep watch on me. If I were not a man I would have the right to complain—or, as it is so cleverly put, register a complaint. I should even, perhaps, be able to present to you a complete diagnosis, even a case history of my illness. But, alas, I am a man, and can do no more than fold my arms across my chest like the Roman and hold my breath till I die. Good night!

DOCTOR: Captain—if you're ill, I assure you it is no dishonor to you as a man to tell me everything. I need to hear your side as well.

CAPTAIN: I dare say having heard one side is quite sufficient.

DOCTOR: No, Captain. You know, when I saw Ibsen's *Ghosts* a few evenings ago, and heard Mrs. Alving deliver a postmortem on her husband, I said to myself: "What a damned shame the man's not alive to defend himself!"

CAPTAIN: And if he *had* been alive? Do you really think he'd have said anything? Do you suppose that any dead husbands come back to life would be believed? Good night, Doctor! As you see, I am perfectly calm, and you can safely go to bed.

DOCTOR: Good night, Captain! I'm afraid I can take no further part in this matter.

CAPTAIN: Are we enemies?

DOCTOR: Not a chance. The pity is that we can't be friends. Good night! *(Goes out.)*

(The CAPTAIN follows the DOCTOR to the door upstage, then goes to the door at the left and opens it slightly.)

CAPTAIN: Come in, we'll talk. I heard you eavesdropping out there. *(LAURA enters, embarrassed. The CAPTAIN sits down at his desk.)* It may be late, but we need to talk this out. Sit down. *(Pause.)* I went to the post office this evening to pick up some letters. It is perfectly clear from them that you have interfered with both my outgoing and incoming correspondence.

The consequence of which is that the time loss has all but destroyed the results of my research.

LAURA: I did it with the best of intentions. You were neglecting your other duties.

CAPTAIN: Best of intentions? Hardly! You knew very well that one day my research would win me more honor than I should ever have had from my military service, and you were determined that I should not distinguish myself, because it could only emphasize your own insignificance. And therefore I have intercepted letters belonging to you.

LAURA: Nobly done!

CAPTAIN: Thank you! I appreciate that! Now, I gather from these letters that you have for some time been working to turn all of my former friends against me by spreading rumors regarding my mental condition. And your efforts have been rewarded, for no one from the commanding officer down to the cook believes me to be sane. As for the facts concerning my illness, they are these. My capacity to reason, as you are aware, is unaffected, and so I am fit to fulfill my duties both as a military man and as a father. As for my emotions, they are more or less under my control, and will remain so as long as my willpower continues relatively intact. You, however, have gnawed and gnawed at it so vehemently that the worn cogs will soon slip their wheel and the entire mechanism fly out of control. I don't intend to appeal to your feelings, since you have none—and that is your strength—but I will appeal to your self-interest.

LAURA: I'm listening.

CAPTAIN: Your behavior has succeeded in rousing my suspicions to where my judgment is blunted and my thoughts have begun to wander—the very event you've waited for—my approaching insanity that can arrive at any moment. You are now faced with the question: Is it more to your interest that I be of sound or unsound mind. Think about it! If I collapse, I lose my job, and you will find yourself in a very awkward position. If I die, you get my insurance. If, however, I kill myself, you get nothing. Logic suggests that you have more to gain if I live out my life.

LAURA: Is this a trap?

CAPTAIN: Yes! It's up to you whether you skirt the issue or approach it head-on.

LAURA: You say you'll kill yourself. You won't.

CAPTAIN: Don't be too sure! How can a man live when he has nothing and no one to live for?

LAURA: Then you capitulate?

CAPTAIN: No, I suggest peace.

LAURA: Your conditions?

CAPTAIN: That I keep my sanity. Free me of my suspicions and I lay down my arms.

LAURA: What suspicions?

CAPTAIN: About Bertha's parentage.

LAURA: Are there any doubts?

CAPTAIN: Yes, and you've wakened them!

LAURA: I?

CAPTAIN: Yes, you've dripped them, one by one, into my ears like poison, and circumstances have made them flourish. Free me from uncertainty; tell me outright that it's so, and I'll forgive you in advance.

LAURA: How can I take on a guilt that isn't mine?

CAPTAIN: How can it matter when you know I won't reveal it? What man goes around trumpeting his own shame?

LAURA: If I say it's not true, you'll never be sure; if I say it is, then you'll know. So you're hoping it's so.

CAPTAIN: It's strange, I know. But the one can't be proven, and the other can.

LAURA: You have reasons for your suspicions?

CAPTAIN: Yes and no.

LAURA: What you want most is for me to be guilty so you can toss me out and take full control of the child. But I won't be lured into any such snare.

CAPTAIN: Why would I want to raise another man's child if I knew you were guilty?

LAURA: No, I'm certain you wouldn't. That's why I know you were lying when you said you'd forgive me in advance.

CAPTAIN: *(Gets up.)* Laura, save me and my sanity. You don't understand what I'm saying. If the child isn't mine, then I have no rights over it, and I don't want any—but that's exactly what you *do* want! Or is there more you want? Like power over her with me tagging along behind as breadwinner?

LAURA: Power, yes. What else has this life-and-death struggle been about if not power?

CAPTAIN: Since I don't believe in an afterlife, the child has become that for me, my conception of immortality, the only immortality that has any basis in reality. Take that from me, and you cut short my life.

LAURA: Why didn't we separate when there still was time?

CAPTAIN: Because the child bound us together, and that bond became a chain. How did it happen? How? I never thought about it, but now memories come flooding back, accusing, condemning. We had been married for two years, but had no children. You know best as to why. I took sick and found myself near death. I remember a moment when I was free of the delirium and heard voices in the sitting room. You and the lawyer were discussing the fortune I still possessed. He explained that you would inherit nothing because we had no children, and asked if you were pregnant. I didn't hear your answer. I recovered. And we had a child. Who is the father?

LAURA: You.

CAPTAIN: Me? No! There's a crime buried here that's beginning to smolder, and what a hellish crime it is! You were all bleeding hearts when you freed your black slaves, but you kept the white ones for yourselves. I've worked and slaved for you, for your child, your mother, your servants. I sacrificed my life and career, suffered torture, whipping, sleeplessness, took on myself every imaginable concern for your well-being till my hair turned gray, all so that you could enjoy a life free of care, so that when you were old you could live it all again through your child. And I did so without complaint, thinking that I was the child's father. This is the vilest form of theft, the most brutal slavery. Seventeen years of hard labor, and I was innocent. What can you pay me in return?

LAURA: Now you've gone totally insane!

CAPTAIN: *(Sits.)* It's what you want, isn't it? I've seen how hard you've worked to conceal your crime. I sympathized with you because I didn't know what was troubling you. I've often lulled your evil conscience to rest, thinking I was chasing off a morbid thought. I've heard you cry out in your sleep and not wanted to listen. I remember the night before last—Bertha's birthday. I was still up, reading, between two and three in the morning. You screamed as if you were being strangled: "Don't! Don't!" I pounded on the wall because—because I didn't want to hear. I've harbored my suspicions for a long time, afraid to have them confirmed. This is what I've suffered for you. What will you do for me?

LAURA: What *can* I do? I swear by God and everything I hold sacred, that you are Bertha's father.

CAPTAIN: What good does that do, when earlier you said that a mother can, *should,* commit any crime for her child? I beg you in the name of past memories, I beg you as a man asking for the *coup de grace,* tell me everything. I'm helpless, helpless as a child; I'm crying to you as a child cries to a mother, seeking pity; forget that I'm a man, a soldier who commands man and beast with a single word; all I want, all I ask is the same pity you would show a sick man. I lay down the tokens of my power and beg for mercy on my life.

LAURA: *(Has approached him and put her hand on his forehead.)* What? A man like you crying?

CAPTAIN: Yes, crying, and a man! Hasn't a man eyes? Hasn't he hands, limbs, senses, affections, passions? Isn't he fed by the same food, wounded by the same weapons, warmed and cooled by the same summer and winter as a woman? When you prick us, don't we bleed? When you tickle us, don't we laugh? When you poison us, don't we die? Why shouldn't a man complain, a soldier cry? Because it's unmanly! Why is it unmanly?

LAURA: Cry, then, child, your mother's here to comfort you as she did once. Don't you remember? It was as your second mother that I first came into your life. Your great, strong body was a bundle of nerves, a child that had come into the world either too early or unwanted.

CAPTAIN: Yes, that's how it was. Father and mother didn't want me, and so I was born without a will. When you and I joined our lives I thought I was making myself whole, and so I let you become my will. I, who gave orders in the barracks and on the field, took orders from you. I became dependent on you, looked up to you as a higher, more gifted being, clung to your every word like your innocent child.

LAURA: That's how it was, then—and so I loved you as my child. But then, you know—oh, and you saw it often enough—every time your feelings took a turn, and you stood there as my lover, I was ashamed, and your love was an ecstasy followed by overwhelming guilt, as if I had committed incest. The mother became the mistress! *(She vocalizes disgust.)*

CAPTAIN: I saw, but I didn't understand. When I imagined you despised my unmanliness, I wanted to win you as a woman by being a man.

LAURA: And that was your mistake! The mother was your friend, you see, but the woman was your enemy, and love between the sexes is war. And don't believe I gave, I didn't give, I took—took what I wanted. But you had the upper hand, and I knew it, and I wanted you to know it.

CAPTAIN: No, it was always you with the upper hand. You could hypnotize me so I neither saw nor heard, but only obeyed; you could hand me a raw potato and make me think it a peach; you could convince me your stupidities were flashes of genius; you could have led me into crime, even into the lowest form of vice. You had no sense, no intelligence, and instead of taking my advice you listened only to your own. But when I finally woke and started thinking again for myself, I looked around and saw the outrage my honor had suffered, and all I wanted was to wipe the stain clean with a great act, a deed, a discovery, an honorable suicide. I wanted to join the war, but wasn't allowed. It was then I threw myself heart and soul into science. And now, when I'm about to stretch out my hand to reap the fruits of my reward, you cut off my arm. I'm stripped of honor; I can't live without honor; a man can't live without honor.

LAURA: And a woman?

CAPTAIN: Yes; she has her children, he doesn't.—We, all of us, ourselves, other people, men, women, have lived our lives as innocently as children, full of imagination, ideals, illusions, and then wakened. And that was fine. Except that we woke all turned around, with our feet on the pillow, and the one who woke us was himself a sleepwalker. When women grow old and cease to be women, they get beards—I wonder what men get when they cease to be men? Those of us who once crowed to make the sun rise were no longer cocks but capons whose calls were answered by sexless hens, so that when we thought the sun was about to rise we found ourselves sitting in bright moonlight surrounded by ruins, just as in the good old days. A morning nap, a crazy dream, and no waking.

LAURA: You know, you should have been a poet.

CAPTAIN: Who knows!

LAURA: But now I'm tired. If you have any more fantasies, save them for morning.

CAPTAIN: Just one more word—and this time not a fantasy. Do you hate me?

LAURA: Sometimes. When you're a man.

CAPTAIN: This is like race hatred. If it's true that we're descended from the apes, then it must have been from two different species. We aren't like each other.

LAURA: What are you trying to say?

CAPTAIN: That in this war one of us will have to go under.

LAURA: Which one?

CAPTAIN: The weaker, naturally.

LAURA: And the stronger is in the right?

CAPTAIN: Always. He has the power.

LAURA: Then I'm in the right.

CAPTAIN: You already have the power, then?

LAURA: Yes. And tomorrow I'll have it legally, when I have you certified.

CAPTAIN: Certified?

LAURA: And then I'll bring up my child as I want, without your wild ramblings.

CAPTAIN: And who will pay for that when I'm no longer here?

LAURA: Your pension.

CAPTAIN: *(Goes menacingly toward her.)* How will you have me certified?

LAURA: *(Taking out a letter.)* This letter. An attested copy is now in the hands of the authorities.

CAPTAIN: What letter?

LAURA: *(Pulling back toward the door on the left.)* Yours! Your letter to the doctor informing him that that you are insane! *(The CAPTAIN looks at her in silence.)* Your function as father and breadwinner is over. An unfortunately necessary function. But now you're not needed. You can go. Especially since you realize now that my mind is every bit the equal of my will. And that, my dear, is a fact that you will never accept. So—go! *(The CAPTAIN goes to the table, takes the lighted lamp, and throws it at LAURA who has retreated backward through the door.)*

END OF ACT II

ACT THREE

There is another lamp on the table. The wallpapered door is barricaded with a chair.

LAURA: Did he give you the keys?

NURSE: Give them! Good heavens! I took them from the clothes Nöjd had laid out to brush.

LAURA: So, Nöjd's on duty today?

NURSE: Nöjd, yes.

LAURA: Give me the keys.

NURSE: Yes, but it's just plain stealing. Do you hear him walking up there? Back and forth, back and forth.

LAURA: Is the door secured?

NURSE: No one could break in there.

LAURA: *(Opens the desk and sits down at it.)* Control yourself, Margret. Only calmness can save us. *(Knocking at the hall door.)* Who is it?

NURSE: *(Opens the hall door.)* It's Nöjd.

LAURA: Have him come in.

NÖJD: *(Enters.)* A note from the Colonel.

LAURA: Give it to me. *(Reads.)* Ah!—Nöjd, have you removed all the cartridges from the guns and game bags?

NÖJD: Just as you ordered, ma'am.

LAURA: Wait outside while I answer the Colonel's letter. *(NÖJD goes out. LAURA writes.)*

NURSE: Listen to him! What's he doing up there?

LAURA: Don't talk while I'm writing. *(The sound of sawing is heard.)*

NURSE: *(Half to herself.)* God have mercy! Where will this end?

LAURA: There! Give this to Nöjd. Mother must know nothing of this. You hear?

(The NURSE goes out. LAURA opens drawers in the desk and takes out papers. A moment later the PASTOR enters and sits beside LAURA at the desk.)

PASTOR: Good evening, sister. I've been gone all day, as you know. I couldn't come earlier. This hasn't been a good day.

LAURA: I've never been through such a night and day in my life.

PASTOR: At least I see you're safe.

LAURA: Yes, but just think of what might have happened.

PASTOR: How did it start? I've heard so many different reports.

LAURA: It began with some wild fantasy of his that he wasn't Bertha's father, and ended when he threw a lighted lamp in my face.

PASTOR: How terrible! That's total insanity! What do we do now?

LAURA: Prevent further outbreaks of violence. The doctor has sent to the hospital for a straight jacket. Meanwhile I've written to the Colonel, and now I'm trying to straighten out the finances that he's made such a mess of.

PASTOR: I'm sad to say I'm not terribly surprised. Fire and water always end in an explosion. What have you found in the drawers?

LAURA: *(Opens one of the desk drawers.)* Here's where he's kept it all hidden.

PASTOR: *(Looking through the drawer.)* Good Lord, here's your doll—and your christening cap—and Bertha's rattle—and your letters, and the locket! *(Wipes his eyes.)* He must have loved you very much, Laura, very much indeed. I've never kept such things!

LAURA: I believe he loved me once, but time—time brings about so many changes.

PASTOR: What's this large piece of paper? The deed for a cemetery plot. Well, better the grave than the asylum.—Laura—are you—are you in any way to blame for all this?

LAURA: I? Blame? For a man's going insane?

PASTOR: Well, well. Better to say nothing. Blood *is* thicker than water.

LAURA: What can you possibly mean!

PASTOR: *(Giving her a hard look.)* Listen to me!

LAURA: What?

PASTOR: Just listen! You can't deny that this fits in perfectly with your wish to bring up your child yourself.

LAURA: I don't understand.

PASTOR: I really do admire you, Laura!

LAURA: Me! Hm!

PASTOR: I'm having myself appointed guardian of that freethinker up there. Fact is, I've always thought of him as a weed in our garden.

LAURA: *(With a short, stifled laugh; then quickly serious again.)* You dare say that to me—his wife?

PASTOR: You're strong, Laura! Incredibly strong! And like a fox in a trap, you'd rather bite off your whole leg than be caught! Like a master thief! No accomplices! No conscience!—Take a look in the mirror! You don't dare!

LAURA: I never use a mirrors.

PASTOR: No, you don't dare!—Show me your hand.—Not a single spot of blood to betray you, no hidden trace of poison. A little innocent murder that the law can't get at—an unconscious crime. Unconscious? Remarkable invention! Listen to him, sawing away up there! Take care! If that man breaks loose, he'll saw you to pieces.

LAURA: Does all this talk suggest a bad conscience? Accuse me—if you can.

PASTOR: I can't.

LAURA: You see? You can't! And so—I'm innocent. You see to your ward, and I'll see to mine. The doctor. *(LAURA rises as the DOCTOR enters.)* Good evening, Doctor! At least you'll help me, won't you? Unfortunately there's not much to be done. Do you hear him carrying on up there? Now are you convinced?

DOCTOR: I'm convinced that an act of violence has been committed. The question is, was that act of violence an outburst of anger or of insanity.

PASTOR: Quite apart from the outbreak, you must admit that he suffers from fixed ideas.

DOCTOR: If I may say so, Pastor, I find your ideas even more fixed.

PASTOR: If you are referring to my religious convictions—

DOCTOR: Convictions aside—*(Turning to LAURA.)* It's your decision, madam, whether to have your husband fined and imprisoned, or committed to the asylum. How would you judge his behavior?

LAURA: I can't answer that now.

DOCTOR: Then you have no firm opinion concerning what is best for your family? And you, Pastor?

PASTOR: There will be scandal in either case. It's difficult to say.

LAURA: If he's only fined for the violence, it could happen again.

DOCTOR: And if he's sent to prison, he'll soon be out again. Am I to take it we're agreed? The best for all concerned is that he be immediately treated as insane. Where is the nurse?

LAURA: Why?

DOCTOR: She's to put the straight jacket on him, but only after I've spoken to the patient and given the order. Not before. I have the—the garment out here. *(Goes out into the hall and returns with a large bundle.)* Would you ask the nurse to step in, please.

(LAURA rings.)

PASTOR: Dreadful! Dreadful!

(The NURSE enters.)

DOCTOR: *(Taking the straight jacket out of the bundle.)* Please pay attention. I want you to slip this jacket on the Captain from behind if I should find it necessary to prevent an outbreak of violence. As you see, it has these unusually long sleeves to hinder his movement. You tie them at the back.

These two straps go through these buckles which are then secured to the back of the chair or couch or whatever is most convenient. Will you do this?

NURSE: No, Doctor, no, I can't—I can't do that.

LAURA: Why don't you do it yourself, Doctor?

DOCTOR: Because he mistrusts me. You, of course, would be the most obvious one to do it, but I'm afraid he mistrusts you, too. *(LAURA grimaces.)* Perhaps you, Pastor—

PASTOR: No, I'm afraid I—

(NÖJD enters.)

LAURA: Have you delivered my message?

NÖJD: Yes, madam.

DOCTOR: Ah! Nöjd! It's you! I'm—I'm certain you know the situation around here—what with the Captain ill, his mind unsettled—well, we need your help in taking care of him, you understand—

NÖJD: Anything I can do for the Captain, he knows I'll do it.

DOCTOR: We want you to slip this jacket on him—

NURSE: No, he's not to touch him. Nöjd's not to hurt him. If I have to, I'll do it myself—gently, very gently! But Nöjd can wait outside and help me if I need it—yes, that he can do.

(Loud knocking at the wallpapered door.)

DOCTOR: Here he is! Hide the jacket on that chair, under your shawl, and all of you go out for a moment—the Pastor and I will receive him. That door won't hold out much longer. Go on!

NURSE: *(Going out to the left.)* Sweet Jesus, help us!

(LAURA locks the desk and goes out to the left. NÖJD goes out upstage. The wallpapered door is broken in causing the chair to fall over and the lock to break. The CAPTAIN enters with a pile of books under his arm.)

CAPTAIN: *(Putting the books on the table.)* It's all here, in every one of these books. Which proves I'm not insane! Here, in the *Odyssey,* book one, verse 215, page six in the Uppsala translation—Telemakos talking to Athena: "My mother tells me that he,"—meaning Odysseus—"is my father, but I can't know that for myself. No one is ever certain of his father." And Telemakos had the same suspicion about Penelope, his mother, the most virtuous of women! Beautiful, isn't it? Beautiful! And here we have the Prophet Ezekiel: "The Fool saith: Lo, here is my father, but who can know whose loins have engendered him?" It's all so clear, so clear! And what's this here? Mersläkow's *The History of Russian Literature.* "Alexander Pushkin, Russia's greatest poet, died tormented more by the widespread rumors of his wife's infidelity than by the bullet lodged in his chest as the result of a duel. He swore on his deathbed she was innocent." Ass! Ass! How could he swear to that! So, you see, I *do* read my books!—Ah, so you're here, Jonas! And the good doctor, of course! Have you heard how I replied to an English lady who complained that Irish husbands throw burning lamps in their wives' faces?—"God, what women!" I said. "Women?" she lisped! "Yes, of course," I answered. "When things go so far that a man, a man who loved and worshipped a woman, throws a lighted lamp in her face, then you know—!

PASTOR: Know what?

CAPTAIN: Nothing. No one can ever know anything—only believe. Isn't that right, Jonas? Believe and be saved! Yes, indeed! But I know that one can be damned for believing! I know!

DOCTOR: Captain!

CAPTAIN: No! I don't want to talk to you! I don't want to hear you transmitting like a human telephone everything they're chattering about in there! *In there!*—Tell me, Jonas, do you believe that you're the father of your children? I recall you once had a tutor in the house, one with a very seductive look about him—and people talked.

PASTOR: Adolf—be careful what you say—

CAPTAIN: Feel up under your hair—go on, feel—any lumps there? Mercy, if he hasn't gone pale! Yes, yes, yes, it was talk, only talk! But they talk so *much!* What a ridiculous bunch of curs we are, the lot of us, we husbands! Don't you agree, Doctor? And what's the story with *your* marriage bed? Wasn't there a lieutenant living in your house? Wait—let me see, now—what was his—ah, his name! Of course! His name was— *(Whispers in the Doctor's ear.)* Why, I do believe he's turning pale, too! Don't let it bother you. She's dead and buried, and what's done cannot be undone. I knew him, you know, the lieutenant, and he's—look at me, Doctor—no, no, straight in the eyes—there—he's now a major in the Dragoons. Damn, if I don't believe he's grown horns, too.

DOCTOR: Would you mind, Captain, if we changed the subject?

CAPTAIN: You see! I only have to mention horns, and he wants to talk about something else.

PASTOR: Adolf—you must know that you are mentally ill.

CAPTAIN: Yes, I'm well aware. And if I had the management of your antlered brains for a time, I'd soon have you behind bars, too. Yes, I'm mad. But how did I become so? You don't care. Nobody cares. Would you like to change the subject now? *(Takes the photograph album from the table.)* My God, there's my child! *My* child? Well, there's no knowing that, is there? Do you know what we'd have to do to know for sure? First, we'd have to marry—for appearance's sake, of course—divorce immediately, become lovers, and then adopt the children. That way one is at least certain of having children who are adopted. Is that right? But what good does this do me now? What good, when you've stripped me of my conception of immortality? What good are science and philosophy to me, when I have nothing to live for? What can I do with my life, when I have no honor? I grafted my right arm, half my brain, half my spinal column to another stem, because I believed they would grow together and together create a more perfect tree. And then someone comes along with a knife and cuts just below the graft, leaving me only half a tree. But the other continues to grow with my arm and half my brain, while I waste away and die, because the parts I gave away were my best. I just want to die. Do what you want with me. I no longer exist.

(The DOCTOR whispers to the PASTOR; they go out to the left. BERTHA enters almost at once. The CAPTAIN sits hunched over at the table. BERTHA goes to him.)

BERTHA: Are you sick, papa?

CAPTAIN: *(Looks up dully.)* Me?

BERTHA: Do you know what you did? Do you know you threw a burning lamp at mother?

CAPTAIN: Did I?

BERTHA: Yes, you did! Just imagine, if you had hurt her!

CAPTAIN: What would that have mattered?

BERTHA: How can you be my father if you talk like that!

CAPTAIN: What's that? Not your father? How do you know? Who told you? Who is your father? Who?

BERTHA: At least not you!

CAPTAIN: Still not me? Then who? You seem to know so much! Who told you that? My own—my own child comes and tells me to my face that I'm not her father! Don't you know how you've insulted your mother? Don't you know that if this is true, she's the one who is shamed?

BERTHA: Don't you say anything bad about my mother!

CAPTAIN: That's right, stick together, all of you, against me! It's been that way from the start!

BERTHA: Papa!

CAPTAIN: Don't you ever say that again!

BERTHA: Papa, papa!

CAPTAIN: *(Draws her to him.)* Bertha, my dear, my dear-dear child, of course you're my child! Of course you are, of course, how could you not be? You are! All that other was only sick thoughts, something brought on the wind, like the plague or a fever. Look at me so I can see my soul in your eyes! But I see her soul, too! You have two souls, and you love me with one, and hate me with the other. But you must love only me! You're to have only one soul. Otherwise you'll never find peace. Nor will I. You're to have only one thought, the child of my thought. You're to have only one will, *my* will.

BERTHA: No, I don't want to! I want to be *me!*

CAPTAIN: I won't let you! I'm a cannibal, and I'll eat you down. Do you see? Your mother wanted to eat me, but I didn't let her. I'm Saturn, who ate his children, because it was prophesied that otherwise they would eat *him*. To eat or to be eaten! That is the question! If I don't eat you, you will eat me—and you've already bared your teeth to me. But don't be afraid, dear child; I won't hurt you. *(Goes to his weapons collection and picks out a revolver.)*

BERTHA: *(Trying to escape.)* Mother! Help! Help! He's going to murder me!

NURSE: *(Entering.)* Mr. Adolf, what are you doing?

CAPTAIN: *(Inspects the revolver.)* Have you taken out the cartridges?

NURSE: Yes, I put them away, but sit down, here, and be quiet, and I'll bring them. *(Takes him by the arm and leads him to the chair where he sits dully. She then takes the straight jacket and stands behind the chair. BERTHA slips out to the left.)* Do you remember, Mr. Adolf, when you were my darling little baby boy, and at night I came in and tucked you up in your warm blanket and said your prayers with you? And do you remember how I would get up in the middle of the night to bring you a drink of water? And how I'd light the candle and tell you all those lovely fairy stories when you had bad dreams that kept you from sleeping? Do you remember?

CAPTAIN: Go on talking, Margret, don't stop, it calms my head so.

NURSE: Yes, my dear, but you must listen. Do you remember how once when you were little you ran off with the big kitchen knife to cut out boats and I had to come and get the knife from you by hook and by crook? You were a very foolish little boy, and so we needed to trick you, because you thought we meant to hurt you. "Give me that ugly old snake there," I said, "or it will bite you!" And lo and behold you let me have the knife! *(Takes the revolver from the CAPTAIN's hand.)* And then those times you were to get dressed and didn't want to. I had to coax you and tell you that you would have a coat of gold and that I would dress you like a little prince. *And then I took the jacket that was all of green wool and held it in front of you and said: "In with those little arms!"* And then I said: "Sit very still now so I can button it up the back." *(She has succeeded in getting the straight jacket on him.)* And then I said: "Stand up and walk around a bit like a good little boy so I can see how it fits." *(Leads him to the couch.)* And then I said: "Now you're to go to bed."

CAPTAIN: What's that? Go to bed? When you've just dressed me? Damn you! What have you done with me! *(Trying to break free.)* Damn you, damn you—sly, wily, cunning woman! Who'd have thought you to be so clever! *(Lies down on the couch.)* Captured, shorn, outwitted, and not allowed to die!

NURSE: Forgive me, Mr. Adolf, I only wanted to keep you from killing the child!

CAPTAIN: Why didn't you let me kill the child? Life is hell and death is heaven and children belong to heaven.

NURSE: How can you know what comes after death?

CAPTAIN: It's all we can know. It's life we know nothing about. If only we'd known that from the beginning!

NURSE: Mr. Adolf! Humble your hard heart and pray to God for mercy, it's still not too late. It wasn't too late for the thief on the cross when the Savior said: "Today shalt thou be with me in Paradise."

CAPTAIN: Are you croaking for the corpse already, old crow! *(The NURSE takes the hymnbook from her pocket. The CAPTAIN shouts.)* Nöjd! Are you there, Nöjd! *(NÖJD enters.)* Throw this woman out! She wants to suffocate me with her prayers! Throw her out the window, the chimney, anywhere!

NÖJD: *(Looks at the NURSE.)* Bless you, Captain, God bless you, but I can't do that! I just can't! Six men, sure, but not a woman!

CAPTAIN: Can't manage a woman, eh!

NÖJD: I can do that, all right. But there's something special keeps a man from laying hands on a woman.

CAPTAIN: Special! Haven't they laid hands on me?

NÖJD: It's just that I can't, Captain! It's about the same as asking me to beat up on the Pastor here. It's something inside—like religion. I can't.
(LAURA enters and signals to NÖJD to leave. NÖJD goes off.)

CAPTAIN: Omphale! Omphale! You play with his club while Hercules winds your wool.

LAURA: *(Goes to the couch.)* Adolf! Look at me! Do you actually believe I'm your enemy?

CAPTAIN: Yes, I believe it. I believe that you are all my enemies. My mother, who didn't want me to be born because my birth would cause her pain, was my enemy. She deprived the embryo of me its nourishment so that I came into the world half crippled. My sister was my enemy when she taught me to be obsequious to her. The first woman I made love to was my enemy for giving me ten years of disease as a reward for the love I gave her. My daughter was my enemy when she was made to choose between me and you. And you, my wife, were my mortal enemy for not leaving me until you had sucked the life out of me.

LAURA: I don't know that I've ever thought of or intended what you think I've done. It's possible there was some dim desire to be rid of you as a hindrance, but if you're looking for a plan in my action, it's possible there was one, even though I wasn't aware. I've never reflected on my actions, everything simply rolled along on tracks you yourself laid down, and before God and my conscience I consider myself innocent, even though I may not be. Your existence has been like a stone on my heart, pressing and pressing until I had to shake off the terrible weight. That's how it is, and if I've hurt you without meaning to, I ask your forgiveness.

CAPTAIN: That sounds plausible enough. But what good does it do me? And who's to blame? Perhaps just the concept of marriage. In the old days a man married a wife; now he enters a business partnership with a career woman, or moves in with a woman friend. He then either fucks the partner or rapes the friend. What's become of love—good, healthy, sensual love? It died in the process. And what is the offspring of this love figured in shares payable to the bearer without joint responsibility? Who is the bearer when the crash comes? Who is the physical father of the spiritual child?

LAURA: As for your suspicions about the child—they're completely unfounded.

CAPTAIN: Yes, and that's what's so terrible! If they were true, there would be something to hold on to, but as it is, they're only shadows hiding in bushes that stick their heads out to laugh. It's like fighting thin air, a mock battle fought with blank cartridges. The real thing, the true betrayal, the fatal reality would have roused me to action with every nerve in my body and soul, but now—my thoughts dissolve into mist and my brain grinds empty till it catches fire. Give me a pillow for under my head. And throw something over me, I'm freezing! Freezing to death!

(LAURA takes her shawl and lays it over him. The NURSE goes out to get a pillow.)

LAURA: Give me your hand as a friend.

CAPTAIN: My hand? The hand you've tied behind my back? Omphale! Omphale! But I feel your soft shawl against my mouth, as warm and soft as your arm that smells of vanilla, as your hair used to when you were young. Laura—when you were young, and we walked in the birch forest with its cowslips and thrushes—beautiful, so beautiful! How beautiful life was, and look what it's come to now. You didn't want this, I didn't want it, and yet it's here. Who rules our lives?

LAURA: God alone rules—

CAPTAIN: The God of Battles, then! Or the goddess, these days. Take away the cat—the one lying on my chest—take it away. *(The NURSE enters with the pillow and takes away the shawl.)* Give me my army coat. Lay it over me. *(The NURSE takes the military overcoat from the clothes tree and places it over him.)* Ah, my coarse lion's skin that you wanted to take from me, Omphale, Omphale! The cunning woman, the friend of peace, the first to disarm men! Awake, Hercules, before they cheat you of your club! You also wanted to trick us out of our armor, pretending it was only frills. No, it was iron before it became frills. The blacksmith used to make it, now it's the seamstress. Omphale! Omphale! Brute strength has fallen to treacherous weakness! Devilish whore of a woman! I spit on you! Your whole damned sex go to hell! *(He raises himself to spit, then falls back onto the couch.)* What's this pillow you've brought me, Margret! It's so hard and cold, so cold. Come, sit beside me here, on the chair. There, that's right. Can I lay my head in your lap? Like that! Ah! So warm! Lean over me so I can feel your breast against me. How sweet it is to fall asleep at a woman's breast—mother or mistress—but sweetest of all, the mother!

LAURA: Do you want to see your child, Adolf? Tell me.

CAPTAIN: My child? A man has no children. Only women have children. It's why the future is theirs. Men die childless. Now I lay me down to—

NURSE: Listen! He's praying to God!

CAPTAIN: No, to you, to lull me to sleep. I'm tired, so tired. Good night, Margret, and blessed be thou among women—*(He raises himself, then falls back into the NURSE's lap with a short cry.)*

LAURA: *(Goes to the door at the left and calls in the DOCTOR who enters with the PASTOR.)* Help us, Doctor, if it isn't too late! Look, he's stopped breathing!

DOCTOR: *(Taking the CAPTAIN's pulse.)* He's had a stroke.

PASTOR: Is he dead?

DOCTOR: No, he might start breathing again, but what sort of life that would be, there's no telling.

PASTOR: "Once to die, but after this the judgment—"

DOCTOR: No judgments! No accusations! You who believe a god guides our destinies will have to take that up with him.

NURSE: Oh, Pastor, he prayed to God in his last moments!

PASTOR: *(To LAURA.)* Is that true?

LAURA: It's true.

DOCTOR: In which case, my science is at an end. It's your turn now, Pastor.

LAURA: And that's it? Is that all you have to say at a man's deathbed?

DOCTOR: That's it. I know no more. If anyone does, it's for him to speak.

BERTHA: *(Enters from the left and runs to her mother.)* Mother! Mother!

LAURA: My child! My *own* child!

PASTOR: Amen!

END OF PLAY

MISS JULIE

A Naturalistic Tragedy

1888

CAST OF CHARACTERS

MISS JULIE *twenty-five years old*
JEAN *valet, thirty years old*
KRISTIN *cook, thirty-five years old*
CHORUS *a party of country people*

SETTING

The action takes place in the kitchen of the Count's house
on Midsummer Night.

Miss Julie

A large kitchen whose side walls and ceiling are hidden by drapes and borders. The rear wall rises diagonally across the stage from left to right. On the left side of this wall are two shelves edged with scalloped paper and full of utensils made of copper, bronze, iron, and pewter. A bit to the right, three-quarters of a large arched exit with two glass doors, through which are seen a fountain with a cupid, lilac bushes in bloom, and the tops of Lombardy poplars. Stage left, the corner of a large, tiled cooking stove with its smoke-hood. Stage right, one end of the servants' dining table of white pine along with several chairs. The stove is decorated with birch leaves, and juniper twigs are strewn on the floor. At the end of the table stands a Japanese spice jar with lilac blossoms. An icebox, a sink, a washstand. Above the door hangs a large old-fashioned bell, and to its left a speaking tube. KRISTIN is at the stove frying something in a frying pan. She wears a light cotton dress and a kitchen apron. JEAN enters dressed in livery and carrying a large pair of riding boots with spurs that he puts on the floor where they remain in view.

JEAN: I swear Miss Julie's gone crazy again tonight! Totally crazy!

KRISTIN: You certainly took your time getting back!

JEAN: Well, I stopped off at the barn after taking the Count to the station. Thought I could do with a dance or two. And there was Miss Julie— leading the dance with the gamekeeper. Seconds later, she was all over me, asking me to dance the ladies' waltz with her. Hasn't let up since! I never saw the like! She's crazy!

KRISTIN: Nothing new for her. Especially the last two weeks, since her engagement was broken off.

JEAN: Right, what was that all about? A good man, too, even if he wasn't rich. Women and their crazy notions! *(Sits at the end of the table.)* Kind of strange, though, don't you think? A young lady choosing to stay home with the servants, rather than visit relations with her father?

KRISTIN: Embarrassed, probably, by that to-do with the fiancé.

JEAN: I guess. He had backbone, though, I have to give him that. You know how it happened, Kristin? I saw the whole thing, you know, but thought better not to let on.

KRISTIN: You what? You saw it?

JEAN: I sure did! One evening I saw them down in the stable yard and she was "training" him, as she put it—you know? I mean, she was making him jump over her riding crop like she was training a dog. He jumped over twice and got a cut from her each time; the third time he grabbed the crop out of her hand and brought it down hard across her face. Hasn't been seen since.

KRISTIN: Hm! So that's what happened! And you saw it!

JEAN: That's how it was, all right! But what are you cooking up there to tempt me with, Kristin?

KRISTIN: *(Serves from the pan and puts it in front of him.)* Oh, just a piece of kidney I cut from the veal roast.

JEAN: *(Smelling the food.)* Ah! Wonderful! Delicious! *(Feeling the plate.)* But you really might have warmed the plate, you know.

KRISTIN: You're harder to please than the Count, I swear! *(Pulls his hair affectionately.)*

JEAN: *(Angrily.)* Don't pull my hair! You know how sensitive I am.

KRISTIN: Now, now! It was only a little love-pull. *(Opens a bottle of beer while JEAN eats.)*

JEAN: Beer on Midsummer Eve! Thank you, no! I've got something better! Right in here! *(Opens a table drawer and pulls out a bottle of red wine with yellow sealing wax on the cork.)* See that? Yellow seal! Give me a glass— no, a wine glass—this is the real stuff!

KRISTIN: *(Goes back to the stove and puts on a small pan.)* God save the woman who gets you for a husband! What an old fussbudget!

JEAN: Listen to her! Get a man as good as me, and you'd be lucky! And it hasn't hurt your reputation any them calling me your boyfriend! *(Tastes the wine.)* Ah! Mm! Very good! Just not quite room temperature. *(Warms the glass with his hands.)* This one we bought in Dijon. Four francs the liter, unbottled, plus duty. What're you cooking there? Smells like hell!

KRISTIN: Some damn concoction Miss Julie wants for Diana.

JEAN: Choose your words more carefully, Kristin. But why stand there cooking for that bitch of a dog on Midsummer Eve? Is she sick?

KRISTIN: She's sick, all right! Stole out one night with the gamekeeper's mutt, and now there's trouble—and that's one thing the young miss just doesn't want to handle.

JEAN: Our "young miss" is too stuck-up in some ways, if you ask me, and not proud enough in others. Just like the Countess when she was alive. She was most at home in the kitchen and the stables. All the same, one horse was never enough to draw her carriage for her. Dirty cuffs most of the time, yet every button was stamped with her coat of arms. Back to Miss Julie, though—she could take a lesson in self-respect—remember her position for a change. A little refinement is in order, to come right down to it. Just now, dancing in the barn? She grabbed the gamekeeper away from Anna and forced him to dance with her. We don't do things like that. But that's the way it is when aristocrats try to come down off their pedestals—they just go downright common! But she's magnificent, all right, no question! Figure—shoulders—etcetera, etcetera!

KRISTIN: I wouldn't overdo it if I was you. Just don't overdo it, you hear? I've heard Klara talk—and she dresses her. She should know.

JEAN: Klara, ah! You women are all jealous of each other! I've been out riding with her! And you should see her dance!

KRISTIN: Will you dance with me when I'm done here?

JEAN: Sure—why not?

KRISTIN: Promise?

JEAN: Promise! What I say, I do, and I will. Thanks for the food! It was the best! *(Puts the cork in the bottle.)*

MISS JULIE: *(Appears in the doorway, speaking to someone outside.)* I'll be right back—you wait there—*(JEAN quickly replaces the bottle in the table drawer and rises respectfully. MISS JULIE enters and goes to KRISTIN at the stove.)* Well, is it ready?

KRISTIN: *(Signals to her that JEAN is present.)* Mm —

JEAN: *(Gallantly.)* I see the ladies will have their little secrets.

MISS JULIE: *(Flips her handkerchief in his face.)* Curious?

JEAN: Ah, lovely! The smell of violets —

MISS JULIE: *(Coquettishly.)* Impertinence! You know all about perfumes now, do you? You certainly do dance well! Now, now, no peeking! Shoo—

JEAN: *(Boldly but politely.)* A witches' brew to work magic on Midsummer Eve? A peek into the future for that future husband!

JULIE: *(Sharply.)* You'd need awfully good eyes to see *that!* *(To KRISTIN.)* Pour it into a bottle and cork it well. Come and dance a schottische with me now, Jean—

JEAN: *(Hesitantly.)* I don't mean to be impolite, but I promised this one to Kristin—

MISS JULIE: Oh, she can dance another one with you—can't you, Kristin? You'll lend me Jean, won't you?

KRISTIN: That's not for me to say, Miss. If Miss Julie condescends to dance, it's hardly for him to say no. You go on, Jean, and be grateful to Miss Julie for the honor.

JEAN: If I can speak frankly, Miss Julie, without meaning to hurt you, of course, I wonder if it's a good idea to dance twice in a row with the same partner, considering the way people talk—

MISS JULIE: *(Flaring up.)* Talk? What do you mean, talk!

JEAN: *(Submissively.)* Since you choose not to understand, Miss Julie, I'll have to speak more plainly. It doesn't look good to show a preference for one servant when they all hope to be similarly honored—

MISS JULIE: Preference! What an idea! I'm amazed! I, the mistress of the house, honor my servants' dance with my presence, and when I want to dance, I want to dance with someone who knows how to lead, and not with someone who'll make me look a fool!

JEAN: Whatever you say, Miss Julie. I'm at your command.

MISS JULIE: *(Softly.)* You needn't take it as a command. It's a holiday! We're celebrating! We're happy! Rank should be set aside. So give me your arm! Don't worry, Kristin! I won't steal your beau! *(Takes JEAN's offered arm and is led out.)*

(The following scene is played in pantomime, as if the actress were really alone. When necessary, she should turn her back to the audience, not look in their direction, nor hurry as if afraid they are becoming impatient.— KRISTIN is alone. Faint violin music is heard in the distance: a schottische. She hums the tune as she clears the table after Jean, washes the plate at the sink, dries it and places it in the cupboard. She then removes her apron, pulls a small mirror out of one of the table drawers, leans it against the jar containing the lilacs, lights a candle and heats a curling iron with which she curls the hair falling over her forehead. She then goes to the door and stands listening. Returning to the table, she notices the handkerchief forgotten by Miss Julie; picks it up and smells it; then, without thinking, spreads it out, smoothes it, folds it twice, etc.)

JEAN: *(Enters alone.)* She's wild! That's all there is to it! What a way to dance! People watching and grinning from behind doors—! What's got into her, Kristin!

KRISTIN: Oh, she's having her period, and that always makes her crazy. How about that dance?

JEAN: You mad at me for dancing that last one with her?

KRISTIN: Of course not. A little thing like that! Besides, I know my place—

JEAN: *(Puts his arm around her waist.)* You've got a good head on your shoulders, Kristin. You'd make a good wife.

MISS JULIE: *(Enters; unpleasantly surprised; with forced joviality.)* Some gentleman you are—running out on your partner like that—

JEAN: Beg to differ, Miss Julie. As you can see, I hurried back to the partner I deserted.

MISS JULIE: *(Changing her tone.)* Nobody dances like you, Jean. I guess you know that, though. But why are you in uniform on a holiday? Take it off at once!

JEAN: In which case I'll ask you to step out for a moment, Miss Julie—my black coat's hanging over here in—*(Gestures as he goes right.)*

MISS JULIE: Do I embarrass you? You're only changing your coat! Well, then, go to your room and come back. Or stay, and I'll turn my back.

JEAN: With your permission, Miss Julie. *(Goes off right; his arm visible while changing coats.)*

MISS JULIE: *(To KRISTIN.)* Tell me, Kristin. Is Jean your fiancé? He's so familiar around you.

KRISTIN: Fiancé? Yes, if you like. We call it that, too, I guess.

MISS JULIE: Call?

KRISTIN: Yes, well, you've been engaged yourself, Miss Julie—

MISS JULIE: Yes, but *properly*—

KRISTIN: Still—it didn't come to anything, did it—?

(JEAN enters wearing a black cutaway and a black bowler.)

MISS JULIE: *Très gentil, monsieur Jean! Très gentil!*

JEAN: *Vous voulez plaisanter, madame!*

MISS JULIE: *Et vous voulez parler français!* Where did you learn that?

JEAN: Switzerland. I was the wine steward in one of the biggest hotels in Lucerne.

MISS JULIE: You're quite the gentleman in those tails! *Charmant! (Sits at the table.)*

JEAN: You're just flattering me!

MISS JULIE: *(Annoyed.)* Flattering you?

JEAN: My natural modesty forbids me to believe that you would actually compliment someone like me. I therefore took the liberty of assuming that you were exaggerating—or, as we call it, flattering.

MISS JULIE: Wherever did you learn to talk like that? You must have spent a lot of evenings at the theater.

JEAN: That, too. Yes, I've been around. Seen many places.

MISS JULIE: But you were born in the neighborhood, weren't you?

JEAN: My father was a tenant farmer on the estate next to yours. You never noticed me, of course, but I saw you often when I was a child.

MISS JULIE: No, really!

JEAN: Yes, and one time in particular—well, except I can't tell you about that.

MISS JULIE: Oh, of course you can! Come on! Make an exception!

JEAN: No, I'm afraid not. Some other time, perhaps.

MISS JULIE: Some other time means never. Why is now so dangerous?

JEAN: Not dangerous, no—I'm just not in the mood.—Look at her! *(Pointing at KRISTIN who has fallen asleep on the chair by the stove.)*

MISS JULIE: What a charming wife she'll make. Perhaps she even snores.

JEAN: Not really. But she does talk in her sleep.

MISS JULIE: *(Cynically.)* How do you know that?

JEAN: *(Coolly.)* I've heard her.

MISS JULIE: *(After a pause, during which they look at one another.)* Won't you sit?

JEAN: Oh, I couldn't, ma'am, not in your presence.

MISS JULIE: If I order you?

JEAN: Then I obey.

MISS JULIE: Well, then, sit down. No, wait. I'd like something to drink first.

JEAN: I'm not sure what's in the icebox. Only beer, I think.

MISS JULIE: "Only"? My tastes are very simple. I prefer it to wine.

JEAN: *(Takes a bottle of beer from the icebox, opens it and looks for a glass and plate in the cupboard; serves her.)* There you are!

MISS JULIE: Thank you! Won't you have some?

JEAN: I don't care much for beer, but if that's an order—

MISS JULIE: Order? Surely a gentleman doesn't let a lady drink alone—

JEAN: I stand corrected—*(Opens a bottle and gets a glass.)*

MISS JULIE: Now drink to my health! *(JEAN hesitates.)* Why, I do believe he's shy!

JEAN: *(Kneels in a parody of the romantic manner, and raises his glass.)* To my lady's health!

MISS JULIE: Bravo! Now kiss my shoe and it will all be perfect! *(JEAN hesitates, then boldly takes hold of her foot, kissing it lightly.)* Really splendid! You should have been an actor!

JEAN: *(Rising.)* This has got to stop, Miss Julie! Anyone could come in and see us!

MISS JULIE: And?

JEAN: People would talk is what. You should have heard their tongues wagging out there a minute ago—

MISS JULIE: What were they saying, I wonder? Tell me. Sit down—

JEAN: *(Sits.)* I wouldn't want to hurt your feelings, but they were saying things that—well—expressions, you know? Well, I know you know, you're not a child, and when they see a woman drinking alone with a man—and a servant to boot—at night—well—

MISS JULIE: Well, what? It's not as if we're alone. Kristin's here.

JEAN: Asleep!

MISS JULIE: Then I'll wake her! *(Gets up.)* Kristin! Are you asleep? *(KRISTIN mumbles something in her sleep.)* Kristin! Some sleeper!

KRISTIN: *(In her sleep.)* Count's boots polished—water for the coffee—right away, right away—mm—pish—ho—

MISS JULIE: *(Taking KRISTIN by the nose.)* Will you wake up?

JEAN: *(Severely.)* Let her sleep!

MISS JULIE: *(Sharply.)* What!

JEAN: Standing over a hot stove all day tires a person out by evening. Sleep should be respected—

MISS JULIE: *(Changing her tone.)* What a considerate thought—it does you credit—thank you! *(Holds out her hand to him.)* Come outside with me now—pick me some lilacs—

(KRISTIN wakens during the following dialogue and, stupefied with sleep, goes out right to lie down.)

JEAN: With you?

MISS JULIE: With me.

JEAN: No, I'm afraid not! We can't do that!

MISS JULIE: I don't understand. Surely you couldn't be imagining—

JEAN: Not me, no, the others—

MISS JULIE: What? That I'm in love with a servant?

JEAN: I'm not conceited, but such things have happened—and for these people nothing is sacred.

MISS JULIE: Goodness, you sound like you're stepping up in the world!

JEAN: Yes, I am.

MISS JULIE: And I'm stepping down—

JEAN: Take my advice, Miss Julie, don't come down. No one will believe you did so of your own free will. People will always say you fell—

MISS JULIE: It seems my opinion of people is higher than yours. Come on, let's see if I'm right! Come! *(Looks tenderly at him.)*

JEAN: You're a very strange person, Miss Julie—

MISS JULIE: Possibly. But so are you. Everything is strange. Life, people, everything—it's all dirt, filth, drifting on the water, drifting till it sinks—sinks—*(Pause.)* That reminds me of a dream I have every so often. I'm sitting on a high pillar, but see no way to get down. When I look down I get dizzy, yet I still have to get down—but I'm not brave enough to jump. I can't continue to hold on, and I long to fall, but I don't fall. I know I'll have no peace until I come down, no rest till I'm down, down on the ground. And if I ever did get down on the ground, I'd want to burrow my way into it—deeply into it. Have you ever felt like that?

JEAN: No. I dream that I'm lying under a tall tree in a dark forest. I want to get up there, up to the top, so that I can look out over the glowing, sunny landscape, and rob the bird's nest up there of its golden eggs. I climb and I climb, but the tree's bark is so thick and smooth, and it's so far up to the first branch. But I'm certain that if I could only make it up to that first branch, I could climb to the top as easily as on a ladder. I haven't reached it yet, but one day I will, even if only in a dream.

MISS JULIE: Here I am, chattering away at you about dreams! Come! Let's dance! Just out into the park! *(Offers him her arm and they start out.)*

JEAN: We'll need to sleep with nine midsummer flowers under our pillow tonight, Miss Julie, so our dreams will come true! *(They stop in the doorway and JEAN puts a hand up to one of his eyes.)*

MISS JULIE: You've something in your eye! Let me see!

JEAN: It's nothing—a speck of dust. It'll be gone soon.

MISS JULIE: It must have been my sleeve. It brushed it. Sit down; let me help you. *(Takes him by the arm and sits him down; takes hold of his head, bends it back, and with the corner of her handkerchief tries to find the speck of dust.)* Sit still now; not a move! *(Slaps his hand.)* Will you obey me or not?—Why, I do believe this great hulk of a man is trembling! *(Feeling his biceps.)* And with such arms!

JEAN: *(Warning.)* Miss Julie!

MISS JULIE: Yes, monsieur Jean?

JEAN: *Attention; je ne suis qu'un homme!*

MISS JULIE: Sit still, do you hear?—There, now, it's gone. Kiss my hand and thank me.

JEAN: *(Getting up.)* Miss Julie! Listen to me! Kristin's gone to bed—Will you listen?

MISS JULIE: Kiss my hand first!

JEAN: Listen to me!

MISS JULIE: Kiss my hand first!

JEAN: All right, but you can only blame yourself!

MISS JULIE: For what?

JEAN: For what! You're twenty-five! You're not a child! It's dangerous playing with fire!

MISS JULIE: Not for me. I'm insured.

JEAN: *(Boldly.)* No you're not! And even if you are—there's highly combustible material in the near vicinity!

MISS JULIE: Which would be you?

JEAN: Yes, not because it's me, but because I'm a young man—

MISS JULIE: Who's highly attractive—handsome! What incredible conceit! A Don Juan, would you say? Or a Joseph? Ah, yes, of course! That's it! He's a Joseph!

JEAN: Am I?

MISS JULIE: Oh, I'm almost frightened! *(JEAN goes boldly to her and puts his arm around her waist to kiss her. She boxes his ear.)* How dare you—!

JEAN: Was that in play or in earnest?

MISS JULIE: In earnest.

JEAN: Then you were serious a moment ago, too. You play too seriously, ma'am, and that's dangerous. But I'm tired of games for the moment. With your permission, ma'am, I'll get back to my work. The Count will want his boots ready first thing in the morning, and it's already past midnight.

MISS JULIE: Forget the boots.

JEAN: Sorry, ma'am, it's my job, I don't have a choice. But I do have a choice about being your plaything, and I choose not—it's beneath me.

MISS JULIE: Aren't we proud!

JEAN: In some ways—not in others.

MISS JULIE: Have you ever been in love?

JEAN: We don't use that word. But, yes, I've been fond of quite a few girls. I was sick once not to have the one I wanted. Sick, you know, like those princes in *The Arabian Nights* who couldn't eat or drink because of love?

MISS JULIE: Who was she? *(JEAN is silent.)* Who was she?

JEAN: You can't order me to answer.

MISS JULIE: If I ask you as an equal, as—as a friend?—Who was she?

JEAN: You—

MISS JULIE: *(Sits down.)* How amusing!

JEAN: Yes, well, as you say—amusing. This was the story I didn't want to tell you earlier—but now I will.—Do you have any idea what the world looks like from down below? No. How could you? It's like hawks and falcons whose backs we never see because they're always up there floating around high in the sky. I grew up in a tenant farmer's hut with seven brothers and sisters and a pig out in a gray wasteland without even a tree. But from the window I could see the wall around the Count's park with apple trees showing above it. For me, it was the Garden of Eden with evil angels standing guard with flaming swords. But angels or no angels, I and some other boys found our way in to the Tree of Life. But now you find me contemptible.

MISS JULIE: No, not at all—all boys steal apples—

JEAN: You say that now, but you still find me contemptible. In any case—I once got into that Garden of Eden with my mother to weed the onion beds. Not far from the vegetable garden there was a Turkish pavilion shaded by jasmine trees and overgrown with honeysuckle. I had no idea what it was for, but I had never seen a more beautiful building. People would go in and come out. And then one day I saw the door had been left open. I stole inside and saw the walls covered with pictures of emperors and kings, and windows hung with red curtains with tassels. Ah, you're holding your nose—I see you understand. *(Breaks off a sprig of lilac and holds it under MISS JULIE's nose.)* I had never been inside the castle, never seen anything but the church—but this pavilion was much more beautiful; and no matter where my thoughts might wander, they always returned there, to that place. Gradually the desire to experience the full pleasure of that place got the better of me. *Enfin!* I stole inside, sat down, looked around, admired—but someone was coming—I had to get out! There was only one way in and out for the lords and ladies, but for me there would have to be another—so I lifted the lid and—down into the depths I went, and slid out! *(MISS JULIE, who has taken the lilac sprig, lets it drop to the table.)* Then I ran—oh, how I ran!—through a raspberry hedge, a field of strawberries, and ended up on a rose terrace. And there I caught sight of a pink dress and a pair of white stockings. It was you! I lay down under a pile of weeds—*under,* if you can imagine!—thistles pricking me and wet, foul-smelling earth! And I saw you, walking among the roses, and I thought to myself: "If a thief can enter into the kingdom of heaven and be with the angels, then how strange it must be that a poor farmer's child here on God's green earth isn't allowed to enter the castle garden and play with the Count's daughter."

MISS JULIE: *(Sentimentally.)* Do you think all poor children in the same situation would have the same feelings?

JEAN: *(Hesitantly at first; then with conviction.)* Do all poor children—yes—of course! Of course!

MISS JULIE: It must be a terrible thing to be poor.

JEAN: *(Cut to the quick; with strong emotion.)* Oh, Miss Julie!—Oh! There's no way you can know! A dog can lie on a countess's sofa, a horse can have its nose patted by a young lady's hand, but a servant—*(Changing his tone.)* Now and then, of course, there are exceptions—someone with enough of what it takes to lift himself up in the world. But how often does that happen! Do you know what I did? I jumped into the mill-stream with all my clothes on, got pulled out, and was beaten! But the next Sunday, when father and the rest of the family went off to visit my grandmother, I managed it so I could stay home. I washed myself all over with soap and warm water, put on my best clothes, and took off for church where I knew I'd see you. I did see you, and went home determined to die, but beautifully, nothing with any pain to it, pleasantly. Then I remembered that it was dangerous to sleep under an elder bush, and we had a huge one in full bloom. I plundered it of all its leaves and blossoms and spread them out in the oat bin and lay down on top. Have you ever noticed the smoothness of oats? As soft to the touch as human skin—Anyway, I pulled down the lid, closed my eyes, and fell asleep. When I woke, I was a very sick boy. But, as you see, I didn't die. What it was I wanted, I don't know. All I know is, there was no hope of winning you. You symbolized the utter hopelessness of my ever escaping the class into which I was born.

MISS JULIE: You have a really charming way of telling a story. Have you ever gone to school?

JEAN: Some. But I've read lots of novels and seen a good many plays. I've also listened to the talk of cultured people. I've learned most from that.

MISS JULIE: And what about us? Do you stand around listening to our conversations?

JEAN: Of course! And quite an earful I've gathered, too. From up on the carriage box, rowing the boat—once I heard you and one of your girl friends—

MISS JULIE: Is that so? And what did you hear, exactly?

JEAN: Oh, well, I—I really don't think I should tell. One thing surprised me, though, was where you'd learned all those words. When you get right down to it, I guess maybe there's not really so much difference between people and—people, as we think.

MISS JULIE: Shame on you! My class doesn't behave like yours when we're engaged!

JEAN: *(Looking at her.)* Are you so certain! Come, now, Miss Julie, you needn't play the innocent with me—

MISS JULIE: The man I offered my love to was shit.

JEAN: That's what you all say—afterwards.

MISS JULIE: All?

JEAN: I'd say so. I seem to have heard it before on similar occasions.

MISS JULIE: What occasions?

JEAN: The one we just spoke of. The last time—

MISS JULIE: *(Getting up.)* Shh! I don't want to hear anymore of this!

JEAN: Neither did she. Isn't it strange.—Well—if you'll excuse me, I'll go to bed.

MISS JULIE: *(Softly.)* Bed? On Midsummer Eve?

JEAN: Yes. Dancing with that rabble out there really has no attraction for me.

MISS JULIE: Get the key to the boathouse and row me out onto the lake. I want to see the sunrise.

JEAN: Is that wise?

MISS JULIE: Worried, are you? About your reputation?

JEAN: Why not? Why risk being made a fool of, getting sacked without a reference, and just when I'm on my way up in the world? Besides, I have a certain obligation to Kristin.

MISS JULIE: Ah, so it's Kristin now—

JEAN: Yes, but you as well. Take my advice, go upstairs, go to bed.

MISS JULIE: And since when do I take orders from you?

JEAN: This once. For your sake. It's late. Lack of sleep makes one drunk and the head dizzy. Go to bed. Besides—unless I'm mistaken—I hear the others coming to look for me. And if we're found here together, you're lost!

CHORUS: *(Heard approaching from the distance; under the following dialogue.)*
  A lad and a lassie met in a wood
  Tri-di-ri-di ral-la tri-di-ri-di-ra!
  Come said the lassie let's do us what's good!
  Tri-di-ri-di ral la la!

  The lass she lay down beside the laddié
  Tri-di-ri-di ral-la tri-di-ri-di-ra!
  And said let us never be sad said she!
  Tri-di-ri-di ral la la!

Then up she rose and donned her clothes
Tri-di-ri-di ral-la tri-di-ri-di-ra!
And went off sayin' that's how it goes!
Tri-di-ri-di ral la la!

MISS JULIE: I know these people, and I love them just as they love me. Let them come—you'll see.

JEAN: Love you, Miss Julie? No, they don't love you. They take your food and spit at you the minute you've turned your back. Believe me. Listen to them. Listen to what they're singing.—No, on second thought, don't listen.

MISS JULIE: *(Listening.)* What are they singing?

JEAN: Some nasty song about you and me—

MISS JULIE: How disgusting of them! The cowards—!

JEAN: Mobs are always cowardly! And since you can't fight them, the only thing is to run.

MISS JULIE: Run? Where to? There's no way out! And we can't go into Kristin's room—

JEAN: All right, then, into my room. This is no time to bother about conventions. You can trust me. I'm a true, loyal, and respectful friend.

MISS JULIE: But what—what if they look for you in there!

JEAN: I'll bolt the door. And if they try to break it down, I'll shoot!—Come! *(On his knees.)* Come!

MISS JULIE: *(Significantly.)* Do you promise me that—

JEAN: I promise! *(JEAN hurries after MISS JULIE who runs out to the right.) (THE BALLET. Led by a fiddler at the head of the procession, the servants and farm people of the estate enter dressed in their holiday finery and with flowers in their hats. They place on the table a keg of beer and a cask of distilled white Swedish liquor, both of them wound festively with green leaves. Glasses are brought out and they drink. They then form a ring and dance while singing the song heard during their approach. When the dance is finished, they leave, singing. MISS JULIE enters alone. Seeing the devastation in the kitchen, she claps her hands together in frustration, takes out a powder puff, and begins to powder her face. JEAN enters in a state of agitation and high spirits.)*

JEAN: There! You see! You heard them! How can you possibly still think that we can stay here?

MISS JULIE: No, not anymore. But what can we do?

JEAN: Leave here—travel—far from here—

MISS JULIE: Travel? Yes, but where?

JEAN: Switzerland, the Italian lakes. Have you ever been?

MISS JULIE: No. Is it beautiful?

JEAN: Ah! Eternal summer! Orange trees, laurels! Unbelievable!

MISS JULIE: But what will we do there?

JEAN: I'll set myself up in the hotel business! First-class all the way, including the customers!

MISS JULIE: Hotel business?

JEAN: Oh, that'll be the life! New faces! New languages! No worry, no anxiety—no time for it! No sitting around thinking what to do! Work calls out to you night and day: bells ringing, trains whistling, buses nonstop, and money pouring in like a flood! Ah, that's the life!

MISS JULIE: For you, yes. What about me?

JEAN: You? The mistress of it all! The jewel of the establishment! Your looks, your personality will be the guarantee of our success! It couldn't be better! You'll sit in your office like a queen and set your slaves scurrying with the press of an electric bell! Guests will file humbly past your throne and lay their offerings on your table. You have no idea how people tremble when presented with a bill. I'll salt the bills and you'll sugar them with your sweetest smiles. Oh, let's get away from here—let's get away from here, now! *(Pulling a timetable from his pocket.)* Now! On the next train! Malmö by 6:30, Hamburg by 8:40 tomorrow morning, Frankfurt-Basel one day, then on to Como by way of the Gotthard tunnel in—let's see— three days. Three days!

MISS JULIE: It all sounds so wonderful. But, Jean—I need you to give me the strength. Tell me you love me! Put your arms around me!

JEAN: *(Hesitates.)* I want to—but I don't dare. Not in this house, not ever again. I love you—you must never doubt that—do you doubt that, Miss Julie?

MISS JULIE: *(Shy, genuinely feminine.)* "Miss"?—Call my Julie. There are no more barriers between us. Julie.

JEAN: *(Tormented.)* I can't! There *are* barriers between us, barriers that will be there as long as we're both in this house! There's the past and there's the Count! I've never met another person I respect as much! All I need to see are his gloves on a chair and I feel small. I hear that bell up there and I jump like a frightened horse. I see his boots there so proud and stiff and my back bends. *(Kicking at the boots.)* Superstition, prejudice, drilled into us since childhood! But they can be forgotten just as easily! Come with me to another country, to a republic, and you'll see how quickly they'll grovel at my porter's uniform! *Their* backs will bend, not mine! I wasn't born to do that! I'm made of better stuff! I have character! I have guts! Just let me get my hands on that first branch and watch me climb! I may be a servant today, but next year I'll have my own hotel. In ten years I'll be a man of means, and I'll travel to Rumania, and get myself decorated, and maybe—notice I said maybe—end up as a count!

JULIE: Very nice!

JEAN: They sell titles in Rumania, and you'll be a countess! *My* countess!

JULIE: I don't care about such things. I'm leaving all that behind me. Tell me you love me; otherwise—hm—well, what am I?

JEAN: I'll tell you a thousand times—just later. And not here. Above all, let's keep our feelings in check, or we'll make a mess of it. We need to look at this calmly and rationally, like sensible people. *(Takes out a cigar, cuts the tip, and lights it.)* You sit down over there, I'll sit here, and we'll talk as if nothing had happened.

MISS JULIE: *(In despair.)* Dear God, don't you have any feelings?

JEAN: Yes, and no one has more. I've learned to control them.

MISS JULIE: A while ago you kissed my shoe, and now—

JEAN: *(Harshly.)* That was then, this is now, and we have other things to consider.

MISS JULIE: Don't speak to me so harshly.

JEAN: I'm not. But we need to be sensible. We've done something very foolish, let's not do more. The Count could be back at anytime, and before that we need to decide our future. What do you think of my plans? Do you approve?

MISS JULIE: They're reasonable enough, except for one thing. You'd need a lot of capital for something so big. Do you have it?

JEAN: *(Chewing his cigar.)* Do I? That should be obvious! Professional expertise, vast experience, and knowledge of languages! Capital enough, I'd say!

MISS JULIE: That won't even buy your railroad ticket.

JEAN: True! Which is why I'll need a backer to put up the money.

MISS JULIE: Where will you find one on such short notice?

JEAN: That's for you to figure out, if you're planning on coming in as a partner.

MISS JULIE: I couldn't possibly. And besides, I haven't a cent to my name.

JEAN: *(After a pause.)* Well, then, it's off—

MISS JULIE: And—

JEAN: —things stay as they are.

MISS JULIE: Is it possible you think that I'll live under this roof with you as your whore? That I'll let those people out there point their fingers at me and snigger behind my back? Do you imagine I can look my father in the face again after this? No! Take me away from this! From this shame and dishonor! Oh, my God, my God, what have I done? *(Sobs.)*

JEAN: Oh, please, let's not get into that, now! What you've done? The same as all the others before you.

MISS JULIE: *(Screams convulsively.)* And now you despise me!—I'm falling! I'm falling!

JEAN: Fall down to me and I'll raise you up.

MISS JULIE: What terrible power drew me to you? Was it the attraction of the weak to the strong, the falling to the rising? Or was it love? Is this love? Do you know what love is?

JEAN: Do I? Oh, I think so. I've been around.

MISS JULIE: I hate the way you talk, I hate the way you think!

JEAN: That's the way I learned it, and that's the way I am! Don't get nervous on me now and play the grand lady, because we're eating off the same plate, you and I, and you'd better get used to it. So just be a good girl now and come on over here. I've saved something extra special for you. *(Opens the table drawer, takes out the bottle of wine, and pours it into two already used glasses.)*

MISS JULIE: Where did you get that wine?

JEAN: The cellar.

MISS JULIE: My father's burgundy!

JEAN: Not good enough for the son-in-law?

MISS JULIE: And I drank beer! I!

JEAN: That only proves your taste is inferior to mine.

MISS JULIE: Thief!

JEAN: Going to tattle on me?

MISS JULIE: My God! Partner in crime with a petty house thief! Was I drunk? Have I been sleepwalking? Midsummer Eve! The night of innocent games—

JEAN: Innocent—hm—

MISS JULIE: *(Pacing back and forth.)* Is there anyone more miserable—

JEAN: Miserable? After your conquest? Think of Kristin in there. Doesn't she have feelings, too?

MISS JULIE: I had once, but not now. No, a servant is a servant—

JEAN: And a whore is a whore—

MISS JULIE: *(On her knees with folded hands.)* Dear God in heaven, end my life of misery! Save me from this filth I'm sinking into! Save me, save me—

JEAN: I really must confess, I feel sorry for you. Lying out there among the

onions beds and seeing you on the rose terrace—I'll tell you this now—
I had the same nasty thoughts as any other boy.

MISS JULIE: But—you wanted to die for me!

JEAN: In the oat bin, you mean? That was talk—just talk.

MISS JULIE: A lie?

JEAN: *(Beginning to feel sleepy.)* More or less. I think I read it in a newspaper
once. A chimney sweep crawled into a woodbox filled with lilacs because
he'd been charged in a paternity suit—

MISS JULIE: So this is the kind of man you are—

JEAN: Well, I had to come up with something. A line always helps—women
fall for it.

MISS JULIE: Fucker!

JEAN: Cunt!

MISS JULIE: So now you've seen the falcon's back—

JEAN: Oh, I don't know about that—

MISS JULIE: And I was to be the first branch—

JEAN: Except the branch was rotten—

MISS JULIE: I was to be the sign outside the hotel—

JEAN: And I was to be the hotel—

MISS JULIE: Sit behind your counter, lure your guests, salt their bills—

JEAN: No, I'd have done that myself—

MISS JULIE: How can a human being be so filthy?

JEAN: Take a bath.

MISS JULIE: Lackey! Servant! Get up when I talk to you!

JEAN: Lackey's whore! Servant's slut! Shut your mouth and get out of here!
You accuse *me* of being coarse? No one of my kind could ever be as
coarse as you've been tonight! When have you seen a kitchen maid go at
a man the way you went at me? When have you seen a girl of my class
offer herself as you have? I haven't, except among beasts and whores!

MISS JULIE: *(Crushed.)* That's right. Hit me. Trample on me. I haven't
deserved any better. I'm rotten. But help me! Help me get out of this—
if there *is* a way out!

JEAN: *(More gently.)* I'd be unjust to deny my share in the honor of seducing
you, but can you believe a man in my position would ever have given
you a glance if you hadn't invited it? I'm still amazed—

MISS JULIE: And proud.

JEAN: Why not! Though I must confess the conquest was too easy to have
been genuinely stimulating.

MISS JULIE: Hit me some more.

JEAN: *(Getting up.)* No. I'm sorry for what I said. I never hit anyone who's down—least of all a woman. I must admit that, on the one hand, I'm gratified that what dazzled us below is only fool's gold, that the falcon's back is no less gray than its belly, that the smooth cheek is really only powder, that manicured nails can have dirt under them, and that the perfumed handkerchief can be dirty. On the other hand, it hurts to know that what I was striving for wasn't something finer, something more substantial. It hurts to see you sunk lower even than your own cook. It hurts in the same way as watching autumn flowers torn to shreds by rains and turned into muck.

MISS JULIE: You talk as though you were already above me.

JEAN: And so I am. The difference is this—I can make you a countess, but you could never make me a count.

MISS JULIE: My father is a count. And I was born of his blood. And that is something that you can never be.

JEAN: True. But I can be the father of a line of counts—if—

MISS JULIE: But you're a thief. I'm not.

JEAN: There are worse things than being a thief. Besides, when I take a job in a house, I consider myself one of the family, so to speak, a child of the house, and surely a child isn't labeled a thief when he snatches a berry off a bush bent to the ground with its load. *(His passion is again aroused.)* Miss Julie, you're a splendid woman! And much too good for a person like me! You let your emotions get out of hand, and now you're trying to cover your mistake by telling yourself that you love me. You don't. Unless, of course, you were attracted by my looks—in which case your love is no better than mine. But I could never be satisfied if all you loved in me was the animal. And I know I could never make you love me.

MISS JULIE: Are you so sure of that?

JEAN: Do you mean there's a chance? Oh, I could love you, no question about that! You're beautiful, you're refined—*(Goes closer and takes her hand.)*—cultivated, loveable when you choose to be, and once you've set a man's desire ablaze, it isn't likely to go out. *(Puts his arms around her waist.)* You're like hot wine with heady spices, and one kiss from you is enough to—*(Tries to lead her to his room, but she slowly works her way free.)*

MISS JULIE: Let me go!—You'll never get me that way.

JEAN: How, then? By falling to my knees and kissing your shoe? The hell with that! Not get you "that way"? Not by petting, not by pretty speeches, not by planning your future, not by rescuing you from disgrace? How, then?

MISS JULIE: How? How? I don't know! No way! None! I hate you the way I hate rats, but I can't escape you!

JEAN: Then escape *with* me!

MISS JULIE: *(Pulling herself together.)* Escape? Yes, escape—But I'm so tired—Give me a glass of wine—*(JEAN pours a glass of wine. She looks at her watch.)* First we have to talk. We still have a little time. *(Empties the glass and holds it out for more.)*

JEAN: Don't drink so much. It'll go to your head.

MISS JULIE: Would that make a difference?

JEAN: "Would that make a difference?"! It's stupid to get drunk! What were you going to say to me?

MISS JULIE: We have to escape! But first we have to talk. Or rather *I* have to talk, since you've done it all so far. You've told me about *your* life, now I'll tell you about *mine*. We need to know each other thoroughly before we go off together.

JEAN: Excuse me—just a moment—please. Think first about what you're doing. You may regret having told me your secrets—afterward.

MISS JULIE: Aren't you my friend?

JEAN: At times, yes—but don't count on me.

MISS JULIE: I don't think you mean that. Besides, everybody knows my secrets.—My mother wasn't born into the nobility; she came of very humble stock. She was brought up to believe the ideas of her time—equality of the sexes, the emancipation of women, and all that. She also had a decided aversion to marriage. When my father proposed, she refused him, saying she wouldn't be his wife, but that he could be her lover. He made it clear to her that he wouldn't allow the woman he loved to be less respected than he was, and she told him she didn't care what the world might think. When he realized that he couldn't live without her, he accepted her conditions. But his decision caused a rift between him and his circle of friends, and he was left with nothing to do but care for his estate, which was never enough to satisfy him. Then I came into the world—against my mother's wishes as far as I can make out. She wanted me brought up as a child of nature, let to run wild and untended, but even more, I was to learn everything a boy learned, to be living proof that a woman is as good as a man. I was dressed in boys' clothes, and made to tend to horses, but was forbidden to milk the cows. I had to groom and harness the horses and hunt. I even had to learn how to butcher—that was the worst! All the men on the estate were given women's jobs, and women did the men's, with the result that everything fell apart and we ended up the laughingstock of the region. Finally my father came to his senses and rebelled and changed everything back to what it was. He and my mother were married very quietly. Then mother took sick—of what I don't know, but she often had convulsions, took to hiding herself in the attic and the garden, and sometimes didn't come home at all at night. Then came the big fire; you've heard about that. The house, the stables, and the barns went up in flame, under circumstances that strongly suggested arson since it happened the day after the insurance expired. My father's quarterly payment had arrived late due to carelessness on the part of the messenger. *(Fills the glass with wine and drinks.)*

JEAN: Don't drink anymore.

MISS JULIE: Oh, what does that matter? We were penniless, without a roof over our heads, and had to sleep in the carriages. My father had no idea where to get money to rebuild. He'd neglected his old friends, so they'd forgotten him. Then mother suggested he borrow from an old childhood friend of hers, a brick manufacturer who lived in the area. Father borrowed, but wasn't allowed to pay interest, which astonished him. And so the estate was rebuilt. *(Drinks again.)* Do you know who started the fire?

JEAN: The Countess, your mother.

MISS JULIE: Do you know who the brick manufacturer was?

JEAN: Your mother's lover.

MISS JULIE: Do you know whose money it was?

JEAN: No—no, I don't—

MISS JULIE: My mother's.

JEAN: The Count's too, then. Unless there was a marriage settlement.

MISS JULIE: There was no settlement. My mother had a small fortune of her own that she didn't want my father to administer, and so she entrusted it to her—friend.

JEAN: Which he then kept.

MISS JULIE: Exactly! He kept it! All this, of course, came to my father's attention, but he couldn't bring suit, couldn't pay back the lover, and couldn't prove that it was his wife's money. That was mother's revenge for father's having taken over control of the estate. He came very close to killing himself. Rumors circulated that he'd tried, and failed. But he lived. He also made my mother pay for what she had done. Those were five dreadful years for me, I can assure you. I loved father, but I sided with mother because I knew nothing of the circumstances. It was from her I learned to hate and distrust men—she hated the whole sex, as you must have heard, and I swore to her I'd never become a man's slave.

JEAN: But then you got engaged to the lawyer?

MISS JULIE: To make him my slave.

JEAN: And he wouldn't go along with it?

MISS JULIE: Oh, he was willing enough, he just didn't get the chance. I got tired of him.

JEAN: Yes, I saw it—in the stable yard.

MISS JULIE: What did you see?

JEAN: How he broke off the engagement. You can still see it—

MISS JULIE: What!

JEAN: There—on your cheek.

MISS JULIE: That's a lie! *I* broke it off! Did he say *he* did? The bastard!

JEAN: Bastard? I don't think so. So you hate men, Miss?

MISS JULIE: Yes—almost always! But then the weakness comes—overtakes me—nature—the burning that won't stop! When will it stop!

JEAN: Do you hate me, too?

MISS JULIE: Insanely! I'd like to see you shot like an animal!

JEAN: Yes, right, like having sex with an animal. The woman gets two years at hard labor, and the animal is killed. That's the law, isn't it? *(She doesn't answer.)* Problem is, you don't have a gun. So, what do we do?

MISS JULIE: Leave!

JEAN: To torment each other to death?

MISS JULIE: No—to enjoy ourselves a day or two, a week, as long as we can be happy—and—and then die—

JEAN: Die? How stupid! Better to start a hotel.

MISS JULIE: *(Not listening.)*—on Lake Como, where the sun is always shining, and laurels are green at Christmas, and oranges glow on the trees.

JEAN: Lake Como is a foul-smelling rainy hole, and the only oranges I ever saw were in grocers' shop windows! It's a good place for tourists, though—all those villas rented to loving couples. That's some business, that! You know why? Because they take out a lease for six months and leave after three weeks.

MISS JULIE: *(Naïvely.)* Why three weeks?

JEAN: They quarrel, of course. But the rent still has to be paid in full. So you rent it out again to another pair of lovebirds, and so on it goes. There's a lot of love around, even though it doesn't last very long.

MISS JULIE: You don't want to die with me?

JEAN: I don't want to die at all. First, because I like living, and second, because I consider suicide a sin against the Providence that gives us life.

MISS JULIE: You believe in God—*you?*

JEAN: Certainly I do. And I go to church every other Sunday. Frankly, I'm getting a little tired of all this now—I'm going to bed.

MISS JULIE: I see. And you think you're going to get off scot-free? Do you think a man owes nothing to a woman that he's ruined?

JEAN: *(Takes out his purse and tosses a silver coin on the table.)* There! Paid up now, am I?

MISS JULIE: *(Pretending not to notice the insult.)* Do you know what the law provides?

JEAN: Unfortunately, the law provides no punishment for a woman who seduces a man.

MISS JULIE: Is there another way out of this other than leaving here, marrying, and then divorcing?

JEAN: What if I refuse to enter this—misalliance?

MISS JULIE: Misalliance—

JEAN: Yes. For me. My ancestry is somewhat more distinguished than yours. We have no arsonists in our midst.

MISS JULIE: How do you know?

JEAN: Because you can't prove otherwise. We don't keep family records, except with the police. But I looked over your family tree in that book you keep on the drawing-room table. Your first ancestor was a miller, I believe. A miller who let the king sleep with his wife one night during the Danish War. Ancestors like that, I don't have. I don't have any ancestors at all, though I could become one myself.

MISS JULIE: This is what I get for opening my heart to someone so low, for destroying my family's honor—

JEAN: Destroying your—Well, don't say I didn't warn you. Drink makes you talk—and you shouldn't talk!

MISS JULIE: Oh, God, how I regret all this, how I regret it! If you only loved me—

JEAN: For the last time—what do you want? Am I to cry, jump over your riding crop, kiss you, lure you off to Lake Como for three weeks, and then—what? What am I to do? What do you want from me? This is getting to be painful, but that's what happens when you get mixed up with women. Miss Julie. I can see you're unhappy, I know you're suffering, but I can't understand you. My people don't carry on like this; we don't hate each other like this. Love is a game for us that we play when we have time off from work, but we don't have all day and all night free like you do! I think you're sick, Miss Julie, I think you're really sick. Your mother's mind was affected and she poisoned your life.

MISS JULIE: Then be kind to me, Jean. At least you're talking to me now like a human being.

JEAN: Then you have to be human yourself! You spit on me, and then won't let me wipe it off—on you!

MISS JULIE: Jean! Help me! Help me! Tell me what to do, where to turn!

JEAN: Christ, if only I knew myself!

MISS JULIE: I was beside myself, I was insane, but isn't there some way out?

JEAN: Just stay where you are, keep calm. No one knows anything.

MISS JULIE: Impossible! The people know! Kristin knows!

JEAN: They *don't* know, and if they did, they'd never believe it.

MISS JULIE: *(Hesitantly)* But—it might happen again.

JEAN: That's true.

MISS JULIE: What then?

JEAN: *(Frightened.)* What then? My God, why didn't I think of that myself! All right, there's only one thing to do! You have to leave! Now! Alone, not with me, that would give us away! Abroad! Anywhere!

MISS JULIE: Alone? Where? I can't do that!

JEAN: You have to! And before the Count comes back. You and I both know what will happen if you stay. Once you've made a mistake you figure you might as well keep on, because the damage has already been done. You get more and more careless, till finally you're caught. So you have to get away. You can write to the Count later and confess everything, except that it was me. There's no way he can guess that. And I doubt he'll be particularly anxious to find out.

MISS JULIE: I'll go if you'll come with me.

JEAN: Woman, are you out of your mind? "Miss Julie runs off with Valet!" It'd be in all the papers in a day or two, and the Count would never survive it!

MISS JULIE: I can't go, I can't stay—help me, I'm so dreadfully tired— Order me! Get me going! I can't think anymore, I can't act—

JEAN: Do you finally see now what a miserable creature you are—always strutting around, your nose in the air, as if you were the lord of creation! All right! I'll give you orders! I order you to go upstairs, to get dressed, and to come back down here with travel money!

MISS JULIE: *(In an undertone.)* Come up with me.

JEAN: To your room? You're crazy again! *(Hesitates for a moment.)* No! You're
   to go at once! *(Takes her by the hand and leads her out.)*
MISS JULIE: *(In leaving.)* Speak gently to me, Jean—
JEAN: An order always sounds harsh. Do you know how it feels now? Do
   you?
   *(MISS JULIE goes out. JEAN, left alone, sighs with relief, sits at the table,
   right, takes out a notebook and pencil and does some calculations, at times
   aloud. He continues until KRISTIN enters, dressed for church. She carries a
   white tie and a shirt front.)*
KRISTIN: Sweet Jesus! What a mess! What have you been up to?
JEAN: Miss Julie! She dragged the whole crowd of them in here! You mean
   you didn't hear anything?
KRISTIN: I slept like a log.
JEAN: Already dressed for church, I see.
KRISTIN: Yes. You promised you'd come to Communion with me.
JEAN: That's right. Of course. I remember. And you brought my things. All
   right, then. *(Sits while KRISTIN dresses him in the shirt front and tie.
   Pause. He speaks sleepily.)* What's the text for today?
KRISTIN: The beheading of John the Baptist, I should think.
JEAN: That'll go on forever. Ouch, you're choking me! God, am I sleepy!
KRISTIN: That's what you get for being up all night! You're downright green
   in the face. What were you doing?
JEAN: Sitting here gabbing with Miss Julie.
KRISTIN: That girl! When will she learn to behave!
   (Pause.)
JEAN: You know, Kristin—
KRISTIN: Know what?
JEAN: I mean, about her, Miss Julie—it's strange when you think about it—
   about her, I mean—
KRISTIN: What is?
JEAN: Everything.
   (Pause. KRISTIN sees the half-empty glasses on the table.)
KRISTIN: Have you two been drinking together, too?
JEAN: Yes!
KRISTIN: Shame on you! Look me in the eyes!
JEAN: Yes!
KRISTIN: Is it possible! Is it possible?
JEAN: *(After a moment's thought.)* Yes, it is.

KRISTIN: Ugh! I would never have believed it! Never! Shame on you, shame!

JEAN: Don't tell me you're jealous of her?

KRISTIN: Of her? No. If it had been Klara or Sophie, I'd have scratched your eyes out! That's the way it is. Why, I don't know.— But that was still a nasty business!

JEAN: Are you mad at her, then?

KRISTIN: No, but I am at you. That was wrong of you, very wrong! The poor girl! No, I want nothing more to do with a house like this, a house where you can't respect the family any more.

JEAN: Why should they be respected?

KRISTIN: Ah, well, you're the smart one, you tell me! Why would you want to work for people who don't act decently? You'd be lowering yourself to do such a thing, it seems to me.

JEAN: It ought to be some consolation that they're no better than us.

KRISTIN: Oh, I doubt that, I really do. If they're no better, then why should we try being like them? What's there to strive for? And then there's the Count. Think of him. Enough misery in his life for two people. No, I don't want to stay here any longer. Not this house. And with somebody like you, to boot. No, if only it had been that young lawyer, some gentleman—

JEAN: What are you—

KRISTIN: Oh, I know, I know—you're all right in your own way. But still there's a difference between people and people. No, this business with Miss Julie is something I'll never forget. Miss Julie, always so proud and standoffish toward men you'd never dream she'd throw herself at one— and especially one like you! Miss Julie who wanted Diana shot because she'd run off with the gamekeeper's mutt! I'll tell you one thing. Come the twenty-fourth of October, you won't find me in this house any longer. I quit!

JEAN: And what then?

KRISTIN: Yes, well, as long as you bring it up, you might as well start looking for another position yourself, since we'll be getting married.

JEAN: Look? Look for what? As a married man I could never find another place like this.

KRISTIN: I know that. But you could take a job as a porter, or a caretaker in some government office. The pay isn't much, but the benefits are worth it, and then there's the pension for the widow and children.

JEAN: *(Grimacing.)* All that's well and good, but it doesn't suit my style to start thinking about dying for wife and children at my age. I've got bigger plans in store for me than that.

KRISTIN: Your plans! Ha! It's time you started thinking about your obligations!

JEAN: Oh, now, let's don't start in on that! I know what needs doing, so just leave it. *(Listens in the direction of the door.)* There's plenty of time to work everything out. Now, go and get ready for church, and then we'll leave.

KRISTIN: Who's that wandering around upstairs?

JEAN: I don't know—unless it Klara.

KRISTIN: *(Leaving.)* Surely can't be the Count come home with nobody hearing him.

JEAN: *(Frightened.)* The Count? No. Not possible. He'd have rung for me.

KRISTIN: *(Leaving.)* God help us! I've never seen the like of this before—*(Goes.)*

(The sun has risen and is shining on the treetops in the park. During the scene, its rays shift gradually till they shine obliquely in through the windows. JEAN goes to the door and signals. MISS JULIE enters dressed for travel and carrying a small birdcage covered with a cloth that she places on a chair.)

MISS JULIE: I'm ready now.

JEAN: Shh! Kristin's awake!

MISS JULIE: *(Extremely nervous during the following scene.)* Does she suspect anything?

JEAN: Nothing. My God, you should see yourself!

MISS JULIE: What is it? What's wrong?

JEAN: You're pale as a ghost, and—I'm sorry, but your face is dirty—

MISS JULIE: I'll wash it, then. Here—*(Goes to the basin and washes her hands and face.)* Give me a towel—Oh! The sun is rising!

JEAN: And the demons vanish in the glare—

MISS JULIE: Yes, the demons were out in force last night.—But, Jean, listen. Come with me. I have money now.

JEAN: *(Doubtfully.)* Enough?

MISS JULIE: Enough to start with. Come with me. I can't travel alone today. Just think of it—Midsummer Day, a stuffy train, packed with hordes of people, gawking at me—endless stops at stations when all you want is to escape! No, I can't, I can't! And then the memories come flooding in, memories of Midsummer Day as a child—the church decorated with lilacs and birch leaves, dinner at the festive table with friends and relatives—afternoon in the park—dancing, music, flowers and games. Run and run as fast as you can, but the memories follow you into the baggage car—with all the shame and guilt!

JEAN: I'll go with you. But now, right now, this minute. Before it's too late!

MISS JULIE: Hurry, get dressed! *(Picks up the birdcage.)*

JEAN: No baggage! It'll give us away.

MISS JULIE: No, nothing. Only what we can carry on.

JEAN: *(Getting his hat.)* What's that? What have you got?

MISS JULIE: Only my finch. I can't leave her behind.

JEAN: What? Carry a birdcage around with us? Have you lost your senses? Put it down!

MISS JULIE: It's the only thing I'm taking from home, the only living creature that loves me, since Diana deserted me! Don't be cruel! Let me take it along!

JEAN: Put it down, I said. And not so loud. Kristin will hear.

MISS JULIE: No, I'll never leave it in strange hands! I'd rather you kill her!

JEAN: Bring the thing here, then. I'll cut off its head.

MISS JULIE: Yes, but don't hurt her. Don't—no, I can't!

JEAN: Bring it! I can!

MISS JULIE: *(Takes the bird from the cage and kisses it.)* Poor little Serena, are you going to die now and leave your mistress?

JEAN: Will you try not making a scene! It's your future at stake here, for God's sake! Hurry up! *(Snatches the bird from her, takes it to the chopping block, and picks up a meat cleaver. MISS JULIE turns away.)* You should have learned to kill chickens instead of shooting pistols—*(Brings down the cleaver.)* It would have saved you fainting at the sight of a drop of blood.

MISS JULIE: *(Screaming.)* Kill me, too! Kill me! You who can kill an innocent creature without even blinking! I hate you! Hate you and despise you! There's blood between us now! I curse the moment I first laid eyes on you! I curse the moment I came alive in my mother's womb!

JEAN: A lot of good all this cursing will do you! Let's go!

MISS JULIE: *(Going to the chopping block, as if drawn against her will.)* No, I don't want to go yet! I can't! I have to see! Shh! There's a carriage outside! *(Listening while never taking her eyes from the block and cleaver.)* So you think I can't stand the sight of blood! You think I'm weak! Oh, I'd like to see your blood on that block, your brains, your cock swimming in a sea of blood! I'd drink from your skull, bathe my feet in the bloody hole in your chest and eat your heart roasted on a spit! You think I'm weak, you think I love you because my womb ached for your semen, because I wanted to carry your spawn under my heart and nurture it with my blood, bear your children, take your name! Listen, you, whatever your name is! What *is* your family name? I've never heard it! Or don't you have one! I'd be known as "Mrs. Doorkeeper" or "Madame Shithouse"—you dog with my collar around your neck, you lackey with my crest on your buttons! Share you with my cook! My own maid's rival! Oh! Oh! Oh! You think I'm a coward and want to run away! No, no, I'm staying! Let the storm break! Father will come home—find his desk broken into—the money gone. He'll ring the bell—*that* bell—twice for his valet—and then send for the police—and I'll tell everything! Everything! Oh, what a relief to have an end—if only it *is* the end! He'll have a stroke then and die, and that will be the end of us—peace—quiet—eternal rest! The coat of arms will be broken over his coffin—the count's line will be extinct—but the lackey's line will thrive in an orphanage, earn its laurels in the gutter, and end up in jail!

JEAN: Bravo, Miss Julie! Spoken like the blood royal! Now just stuff the miller back in his sack!

(KRISTIN enters dressed for church and carrying a hymn book. MISS JULIE rushes to her, throwing herself into her arms as if seeking protection.)

MISS JULIE: Help me, Kristin! Help me against this man!

KRISTIN: *(Cold and unmoved.)* What's all this nonsense on a Sunday morning! *(Looks at the chopping block.)* Look at that mess! What's the meaning of this? And all your screaming and shouting!

MISS JULIE: You're a woman, Kristin! You're my friend! Watch out for this evil man!

JEAN: *(A bit shy and embarrassed.)* While the ladies are having their heart-to-heart, I'll go have a shave! *(Slinks out to the right.)*

MISS JULIE: You must understand, Kristin! You must listen to me!

KRISTIN: No, I don't understand! I don't understand any of this! And where are you going in those travel clothes? And him with his hat on? What! What's the meaning of this!

MISS JULIE: Listen to me, Kristin, listen—I can explain it all!

KRISTIN: Well, I don't want to know!

MISS JULIE: Please listen!

KRISTIN: To what? To this nonsense you're up to with Jean? I couldn't care less! That's between you and him! But if you're of a mind to talk him into skipping out with you, well, I'll put a stop to that fast enough!

MISS JULIE: *(Extremely nervous.)* Please, Kristin, be quiet, listen to me. I can't stay here, and Jean can't stay here—so we have to leave—

KRISTIN: Hm, hm!

MISS JULIE: *(Brightening.)* No, wait—I've just had an idea—what if we all go away—abroad—the three of us—to Switzerland—and start a hotel! I have money, you see—and Jean and I would manage it all—and—and you, well, I thought you would manage the kitchen! Wouldn't that be just the thing! Say yes! And come with us, and that will settle everything! Oh, say yes, Kristin! *(Puts her arms around KRISTIN and pats her.)*

KRISTIN: *(Cold, thoughtfully.)* Hm, hm!

MISS JULIE: *(Presto tempo.)* You've never traveled, Kristin! You need to get out and have a look at the world! Oh, the fun you'll have traveling on trains! You can't imagine! New people all the time—new countries! And when we get to Hamburg, we'll take in the zoo—you'll like that, won't you—and we'll go to the theater and hear an opera—and then in Munich there'll be all the museums, with Rubens and Raphael, the great painters, you know. You've heard of Munich, I know you have, where King Ludwig lived—the king who went insane—we'll see his castles, too—they're still there, just like in fairy tales! And from there it's no time at all to Switzerland—and the Alps—just imagine, snow on the Alps in the middle of summer! And oranges—oranges and laurels that are green all year long! *(JEAN is seen in the right wing, sharpening his razor on a strop that he holds between his teeth and with his left hand. He listens to the talk with satisfaction, nodding in agreement every so often. MISS JULIE continues tempo prestissimo.)*—And we'll open a hotel there—and I'll sit at the desk while Jean receives the guests—and goes out shopping—and writes letters. That's the life, Kristin, oh, that's the life, believe me! Train whistles blowing, buses driving up, bells ringing upstairs and in the restaurant—and me making out the bills—*and* salting them, I don't mind saying! You have no idea how people tremble when you present them with a bill!—And you, you, Kristin—you'll be mistress of the kitchen!—Naturally, you won't be slaving over the stove yourself—and you'll dress nicely and neatly, because people will see you—and with your looks, Kristin—and don't think I'm flattering you—one fine day you'll catch yourself a husband—some rich Englishman—that kind is so easy to—*(Slowing down.)*—to catch!—And we'll get rich—and build a villa on Lake Como! It rains there occasionally, of course, but—*(More and more weakly.)*—the sun has to shine sometime—even though it looks dark—and—then—or else we can go home again—come back— *(Pause.)*—here—or somewhere else—

KRISTIN: Listen, Miss Julie! Do you believe all of that yourself?

MISS JULIE: *(Crushed.)* Do I believe it myself?

KRISTIN: Yes!

MISS JULIE: *(Wearily.)* I don't know. I don't believe in anything anymore. *(Sinks to the bench and puts her head on her arms on the table.)* Nothing! Nothing at all!

KRISTIN: *(Turning toward JEAN.)* So! You were planning on running away, were you!

JEAN: *(Taken aback, lays his razor on the table.)* Well, I wouldn't exactly call it that! Don't exaggerate. You heard Miss Julie's plan. She may be tired from being up all night, but her plan is still practical.

KRISTIN: Listen to him! Was it your idea I'd be cook for that—

JEAN: *(Sharply.)* You watch your language in front of your mistress! Understand?

KRISTIN: Mistress!

JEAN: Yes!

KRISTIN: Listen to him! Just listen!

JEAN: Listen, yes, and talk a little bit less, if you ask me! Miss Julie is your mistress! If you're going to despise her for what she's done, you ought to despise yourself for the same reason!

KRISTIN: I've always had a high enough opinion of myself—

JEAN: To be able to look down on others!

KRISTIN: —not to lower myself below my station! There's nobody can say the Count's cook went mucking around with the stableman or the swineherd! Nobody!

JEAN: Right! Lucky you! Got herself a regular gentleman!

KRISTIN: A regular gentleman who sells oats out of the Count's stable!

JEAN: Listen to who's talking! Miss Piety here who gets a kickback from the grocer and bribes from the butcher!

KRISTIN: What!

JEAN: And she complains she can't respect her employers! You, you—!

KRISTIN: Are you coming to church or not? You could use a good sermon after what you've done!

JEAN: No, I am not coming to church! Go yourself and confess your own sins!

KRISTIN: I'll do that, yes, and I'll come home with enough forgiveness to go around for both of us! The Savior suffered and died on the cross for our sins, and if we come to Him with faith and repentance, He'll take all our sins upon Him.

JEAN: Does that go for the groceries, too?

MISS JULIE: Do you believe that, Kristin?

KRISTIN: It's my living faith, as true as I'm standing here, the same faith I've had since my childhood, Miss Julie. Where sin abounds, grace abounds also.

MISS JULIE: Oh, if only I had your faith! If only I—

KRISTIN: Yes, but you can't get that without God's special grace, and that's not given to everyone.

MISS JULIE: Who is it given to?

KRISTIN: That's the great mystery of His grace, Miss Julie. God is no respecter of persons. There the last shall be first and the—

JULIE: Then He does have respect for the last?

KRISTIN: (Continuing.)—and it is easier for a camel to pass through the eye of a needle than for a rich man to enter into the Kingdom of Heaven. That's how it is, Miss Julie. I'll be going now—alone—and as I pass by, I'll tell the stableman not to let out any horses in case someone should want to get away before the Count returns. Good-bye! (Goes.)

JEAN: Bitch! And all this because of a finch!

MISS JULIE: (Dully.) Forget the finch. Do you see any way out of this, any way to end it?

JEAN: (Thinking.) No.

MISS JULIE: What would you do in my place?

JEAN: In your place? Let me think. As an aristocrat, as a woman—a fallen woman—I don't know. No, wait—no, I think I might! Yes—

MISS JULIE: (Picks up the razor and makes the gesture of cutting her throat.) Like this?

JEAN: Yes! Except that I *personally* wouldn't do it, you see. That's the difference between us!

MISS JULIE: Because you're a man and I'm a woman? What difference does that make?

JEAN: The difference it makes is the difference there is—between a man and a woman.

MISS JULIE: (The razor in her hand.) I want to. But I can't. My father couldn't, either, that time he should have.

JEAN: No, he was right not to. He first had to get his revenge.

MISS JULIE: And now mother is having her revenge again—through me.

JEAN: Have you ever loved your father, Miss Julie?

MISS JULIE: Oh, yes, enormously! But I must have hated him, too—hated him without ever realizing it. He's the one who brought me up to despise my own sex—made me half a woman and half a man. Who's fault is it what's happened? Father's? Mother's? Mine?—Mine!—I don't even have a *self* I can call my own! I haven't a thought that didn't come from my father, an emotion that didn't come from my mother, and as for that last idea—that all people are created equal—that one I got from my fiancé, and that's why I say he's shit! How can it be my fault? Should I shuffle the blame onto Jesus, the way Kristin does? No, I'm too proud for that, *and* too sensible—thanks to father's teaching! And that bit about the rich not getting into heaven? That's a lie! At least Kristin, who has money in the bank, won't get in! Who's fault is it? What difference does it make whose fault it is? I'll still be the one to bear the guilt, to pay the consequences—

JEAN: Yes, but—*(The bell rings sharply twice. MISS JULIE leaps to her feet. JEAN quickly changes to his livery.)* The Count's come back! What if Kristin—*(Goes to the speaking tube, knocks on it, listens.)*

MISS JULIE: Has he already been to his desk—?

JEAN: This is Jean, sir!—Yes, sir!—Yes, sir!—At once!—In half an hour, sir!

MISS JULIE: *(Anxiety ridden.)* What did he say! For God's sake, what did he say!

JEAN: He wants his boots and coffee in half an hour.

MISS JULIE: Half an hour, then.—Oh, I'm so tired! I can't do a thing. Can't repent, can't run away, can't stay, can't live—can't die. Help me. Order me. I'll obey like a dog. Do me this last service—save my honor, save his name. You know what I *should* do but haven't the *will* to. Order me. Give me *your* will. *Make* me do it!

JEAN: I don't know—I can't, either—not now. Why, I don't know. It's like this jacket won't let me—order you. And now, since the Count has just spoken to me—I—I can't explain it—it's that damned lackey in me! I think if the Count came down here this minute and ordered me to slit my throat, I'd do it, right on the spot.

MISS JULIE: Then pretend that you're him, and I'm you. You were such a grand actor awhile back when you were on your knees to me. You were a real aristocrat then. Or—or have you ever been to the theater and watched a hypnotist? *(JEAN nods ascent.)* He says to his subject: "Take this broom," and he takes it. Then he says: "Sweep," and he sweeps.

JEAN: But the subject has to be asleep.

MISS JULIE: *(Ecstatically.)* I'm already asleep—the whole room is a haze of gray smoke—and you look like an iron stove—that looks like a man in black with a tall hat—and your eyes glow like coals in a dying fire—your face is a white smudge—ashes—*(The sunlight has by now reached the floor and is shining on JEAN.)* It's so good—so warm—*(Rubbing her hands together as if in front of a fire.)*—and so bright—so peaceful—

JEAN: *(Takes the razor and places it in her hand.)* Here's the broom. Go while it's still bright—out to the barn—and—*(Whispers in her ear.)*

MISS JULIE: *(Waking up.)* Thank you! I'm going to my rest now. But tell me one thing—that the first can also receive the gift of grace. Tell me—even if you don't believe it.

JEAN: The first? No, I can't—I can't do that. But wait, Miss Julie—here's what I *can* tell you. I can tell you that you're no longer among the first— you're—you're—one of—the last!

MISS JULIE: That's true! One of the last! The very last! Oh!—But now I can't go. Tell me just once more to go!

JEAN: No, now I can't, either! I can't!

JULIE: And the first shall be the last!

JEAN: Don't think! Don't think! You're draining my strength away—making me a coward! What! I think the bell moved!—No! Should we stuff paper in it?—Scared of a bell!—But it isn't only a bell—there's someone behind it—a hand sets it going—and something else sets the hand going—just cover your ears! Cover your ears! But then it'll only ring louder! Ring and ring till someone answers—and then it's too late! And then the police will come—and then—*(The bell rings sharply twice. JEAN cringes, then straightens up.)* It's horrible! But there's no other way!—Go! *(MISS JULIE walks resolutely out through the door.)*

END OF PLAY

THE STRONGER

A Sketch

1888–89

The Stronger

Two small cast-iron tables, a red plush sofa, and a few chairs. MRS. X enters wearing a winter coat and hat, and with a charming Japanese basket on her arm. MISS Y is seated at a table with a half-empty bottle of beer in front of her; she is reading an illustrated magazine, which every now and then she exchanges for another.

MRS. X: Amelia, darling, really! Sitting here like some lonely bachelor on Christmas Eve!

MISS Y: *(Looks up from the magazine, nods, and continues reading.)*

MRS. X: Really, I feel sorry for you, dear, alone—alone in a café—on Christmas Eve of all times! Almost as sorry, I must say, as a wedding breakfast I once saw in a Paris restaurant—the bride sat reading a humor magazine while the groom was off playing billiards with the best man and the ushers. Goodness, I thought to myself, with such a beginning, how will it all end! Imagine, playing billiards on his wedding day! Yes, and I can just hear you about to respond: "After all, she *was* reading a humor magazine!" Yes, well, it's not quite the same, don't you see. *(A WAITRESS brings a cup of hot chocolate and places it in front of MRS. X, then goes out.)* I hate to say this, Amelia, but I think you'd have done better if you'd kept your fiancé. After all, I *was* the first person to tell you to forgive him. But, then, how could you forget. Imagine, you'd be married now, with a home. Do you remember that Christmas in the country with your fiancé's parents, and how happy you were? How you went on and on about all that really matters is the joy of home and family life, and how you longed to get away from the theater! It's true, my darling, it is, a home is certainly the best—after the theater, of course—and then the children, you know—well, no, I suppose you wouldn't know that, would you, Amelia—

MISS Y: *(Gives her a contemptuous glance.)*

MRS. X: *(Sips a few teaspoons from her cup, then opens the basket to show her Christmas purchases.)* Ah, let me show you now what I've bought for my little sweethearts! *(Takes out a doll.)* Isn't it precious! It's for Lisa. And look! It rolls its eyes and turns its neck! And here's a little cork-pistol for Maja. *(Loads it, aims it at MISS Y, and shoots.)*

MISS Y: *(Recoils in fear.)*

MRS. X: Oh, mercy! Did I frighten you! Did you think I meant to shoot you?—Goodness, I believe you did! I'd be much less surprised if *you* wanted to shoot *me*—considering the obstacles I've thrown in your path—which I know you can never forgive me for—even though I was completely innocent. You still believe, I know you do, that I schemed to get you out of the Theatre Royal, but I did nothing of the sort, yet you insist on thinking so!—Ah, well, what's the point of all this, you're determined not to believe me. *(Taking out a pair of embroidered slippers.)* And these are for my husband. Tulips! I embroidered them myself. Which is odd, because I loathe tulips, but he *will* have them on everything!

MISS Y: *(Looks up from her magazine with a mixture of cynicism and curiosity.)*

MRS. X: *(Puts a hand in each slipper.)* What tiny feet he has. You see? And you should see how elegantly he walks! Ah, but, then, you've never seen him in slippers, have you—

MISS Y: *(Laughs aloud.)*

MRS. X: Look! Here he comes! *(Walks the slippers across the table.)*

MISS Y: *(Laughs aloud again.)*

MRS. X: And when he gets angry, you see, he stamps his foot on the floor, like this. "Damn! Will these maids never learn how to make coffee!" Or: "That idiot girl has forgotten to trim my lamp again!" And when there's a draft on the floor and he gets cold feet: "It's freezing! Can't those fools learn how to keep the fire from going out!" *(Rubs the sole of one slipper against the top of the other.)*

MISS Y: *(Laughs with abandon.)*

MRS. X: And then he comes home and has to hunt high and low for his slippers because Marie has hidden them under the dresser. Goodness, I should be ashamed of myself for making fun of my husband like this. But he's really very sweet, an absolute darling of a husband.—You really should have had one just like him, Amelia! Why, what are you laughing at? Mm? Mm? And then, well, you see, I know he's faithful to me. I know, for he's told me so himself, indeed he has. No doubt about it. Now, whatever are you grinning at? Well, for example, while I was on my Norwegian tour, that nasty little Frederique tried to seduce him. Really, now, can you imagine anything so, so, so brazen! *(Pause.)* I'd have scratched her beady little eyes clear out of her head if she'd come around while I was at home! *(Pause.)* It was a good thing he told me himself.

Imagine hearing it from some gossip! *(Pause.)* Frederique, of course, wasn't the only one. Oh, I just don't know why, but women go absolutely crazy over my husband. They all seem to want him. They must think he has some influence at the theater because he's in the government. Who knows, perhaps even you may have had your claws out for him. I've never quite trusted you, you know. But now, of course, I know that he was never really interested in you. And then there was always that grudge you seemed to hold against him. *(Pause. They look at each other with a kind of edgy uncertainty.)* All right, now, Amelia, look, I want you to come spend the evening with us, just to show you're not mad at us, at least not at me. I really find it terribly unpleasant being on bad terms with people—especially you. Perhaps it was because I got that part that you were so terribly set on—*(Gradually more slowly.)*—or—oh, I don't know—not the foggiest, really, you know—*(Pause.)*

MISS Y: *(Gazes at MRS. X curiously.)*

MRS. X: *(Thoughtful.)* It was so strange—our friendship. The first time I met you, do you know, I was afraid of you—so afraid that I never let you out of my sight. Wherever I went, I found myself always near you. I hadn't the courage to be your enemy, so I became your friend. But there was always something between us, something awkward. When you came to visit, I saw that my husband couldn't stand you—it made me uncomfortable, as when one's clothes don't quite fit. I did everything I could to make him be friendly to you at least, but nothing worked. Not until you became engaged, that is. Then all at once you became such fast friends that it looked as if you hadn't had the courage to show your true feelings before—before you were committed—before it was—safe. Then later— hm—let me see, now! Oh, yes—I didn't get jealous—no, and isn't that strange? And then there was the christening—you were godmother— and I made him kiss you—he did, and it upset you terribly—well, I mean—I didn't notice it at the time—nor did I afterward—I haven't really thought of it—till—this—*moment! (Rises impulsively.)* Why don't you say something? You haven't uttered a single word all this time, just let me go on talking, staring at me, pulling out of me all these thoughts like silk from a cocoon—thoughts—suspicious—? Let me think! Why did you break your engagement? Why did you never come to visit after that? Why won't you come to be with us tonight?

MISS Y: *(Appears as if about to speak.)*

MRS. X: No. Never mind. Better to say nothing. I see it all, now. So that was why. And that! And that! And that! It all falls into place. Shame on you!

I don't want to sit at the same table with you! *(Moves her things to the other table.)* That was why I had to embroider tulips, which I hate, on his slippers, because you love tulips! That was why—*(Throws the slippers on the floor.)*—we had to spend our vacation at Lake Mälaren that summer, because you couldn't stand the salt sea air! That was why my son had to be named Eskil, because that was your father's name! That was why I had to wear your colors, read your authors, eat your favorite dishes, and drink your drinks—chocolate, for example! That was why—oh, God, it's too terrible to think of, too terrible! You forced everything on me, everything, even your passions! Your soul drilled its way into mine like a worm into an apple, and ate and ate, boring and boring, till all that was left was the shell and a little black dust. I wanted to run away from you, but I couldn't. You were always there, like a snake, with your black eyes, bewitching me. I tried to fly, but my wings only weighted me down. I lay in the water, my feet tied together, trying to swim with my hands, but the more I struggled, the deeper I sank, down, down, till I lay on the bottom, and there you were, a monstrous crab waiting to catch me in your claws—and that's where I am now!—I hate you, hate you, hate you! But you—you just sit there, quiet, unmoving, not caring—not caring whether it's day or night, winter or summer, whether other people are happy or unhappy.—You can't hate, you can't love, you know nothing about either—you're a cat motionless at a rat-hole, unable to drag it out, unable to pursue it, able only to outwait it! You sit here in your corner—do you know what they call it, this corner, because of you?—the rattrap!—but here you sit, reading your papers, in search of someone ill or in trouble or fired from the theater so that you can grab up the part. You sit here scrutinizing your victims, calculating your chances like a pilot his shipwrecks, collecting tribute.—Poor Amelia! Do you know, my dear, I really do feel sorry for you—sorry because I know you're unhappy, unhappy as one who has been hurt, and malicious because it does hurt so. Try as I may, I can't be angry with you, because you're so small, you know, so very small, really little more than a babe in arms. And as for that business with Bob, it's really of no importance. I mean, how could it be? And what does it matter whether it was you or someone else who taught me to drink chocolate? *(Sips a teaspoonful of chocolate; then continues with great practicality.)* In any case, chocolate's a very healthy drink! And if you've taught me how to dress—*tant mieux!* It's only made my husband even fonder of me—you're loss has been my gain, as they say. In fact, from all appearances, I'd say you've already lost him. Naturally, you expected *me* to leave *him* and go flying off in my own direction. But as it happened, that's what *you* did, and now you sit here regretting it. I would never do that, you see. But we mustn't be petty. Practically speaking, why should I want what no one else wants?— When all's been said and done, perhaps I've come out of this the stronger—for the moment, at least. You never got anything from me— you simply gave; and so I ended up like the thief in the night: When you woke up I had everything you'd lost!—How else can it be explained? Everything you put your hand to became worthless and sterile. You couldn't keep his or any man's love with all your tulips and your passions. I could. You couldn't learn the art of living with all your books. I did. You didn't give birth to a baby boy you could name Eskil; you only had a father named Eskil.—And why are you always so silent? Never a word! Never a sound! Silence! I used to think it was a sign that you were the strong one. Probably the truth was much simpler: You had nothing to say—because you hadn't a thought in that pretty little head. *(Rises and picks up the slippers.)* I'll be going now—home—and take my tulips with me—*your* tulips! You couldn't learn anything from others—you couldn't bend—and so you broke, like a dry reed. I didn't!—Thank you, Amelia, for all your instruction. Thank you for teaching my husband how to make love! I'm going home now—to love him. *(Goes.)*

END OF PLAY

A Dream Play

1901

As in his earlier dream play, *Toward Damascus,* the author has attempted in this dream play to imitate the disconnected but apparently logical form of a dream. Anything can happen, everything is possible and probable. Space and time do not exist. Based on a slight foundation of reality, imagination wanders afield and weaves new patterns comprised of mixtures of recollections, experiences, unconstrained fantasies, absurdities, and improvisations. Characters split, double, and multiply; they evaporate, crystallize, dissolve, and reconverge. But one single consciousness governs them all, that of the dreamer. For him there are no secrets, no incongruities, no scruples, and no laws. He neither condemns nor does he acquit, he merely reports. And since there is generally more pain than pleasure in the dream, a tone of melancholy and sympathy for all things runs through the swaying narrative. Sleep, the liberator, is often tortuous; and yet when pain is at its worst, the sufferer is wakened and reconciled with reality. For however agonizing reality may be, it is, at this moment, when compared with the torments of the dream, a joy.

CAST OF CHARACTERS

THE VOICE OF FATHER INDRA
INDRA'S DAUGHTER
THE GLAZIER
THE OFFICER
THE MOTHER
THE FATHER
LINA
THE STAGE-DOOR KEEPER
THE BILL-POSTER
A BALLET GIRL
A CHORUS GIRL
THE PROMPTER
A POLICEMAN
THE LAWYER
KRISTIN
THE QUARANTINE MASTER
THE DANDY
THE MALE FRIEND
THE COQUETTE

THE POET
HE
SHE
THE PENSIONER
THREE GIRLS
UGLY EDITH
EDITH'S MOTHER
ALICE
A NAVAL OFFICER
THE SCHOOLMASTER
A STUDENT
THE HUSBAND
THE WIFE
THE BLIND MAN
THE FIRST COAL CARRIER
THE SECOND COAL CARRIER
THE GENTLEMAN
THE LADY
THE CHANCELLOR
THE DEAN OF THE THEOLOGICAL FACULTY
THE DEAN OF THE PHILOSOPHICAL FACULTY
THE DEAN OF THE MEDICAL FACULTY
THE DEAN OF THE LAW FACULTY

ADDITIONAL CHARACTERS: chorus girls, ballet girls, people from the opera company, clerks, ushers, femal dancers, three doctoral candidates, professors of the four faculties, children, schoolboys, and crew—all right-thinking people.

A Dream Play

Wisps of clouds in shapes of crumbling cliffs with ruined castles and fortresses. The constellations of Leo, Virgo, and Libra are seen, with the planet Jupiter shining brightly among them. INDRA'S DAUGHTER stands at the peak of the clouds.

INDRA'S VOICE: *(From above.)* Where are you, Daughter, where?
DAUGHTER: Here, Father, here!
INDRA'S VOICE: You've gone astray, child.
    Be careful, you're sinking.
    How did you get here?
DAUGHTER: I followed the lightning's fiery flame
    from ethereal regions with a cloud for my chariot.
    The cloud sank and is still falling.
    Tell me, great Father Indra,
    what region have I come to?
    The air is oppressive
    and breathing is difficult.
INDRA'S VOICE: You have left the second world and entered the third.
    You have left far behind
    Çucra the morning star,
    and have now entered Earth's atmosphere.
    Take as a sign the Seventh House of the Sun
    known as Libra, where at autumn's beginning
    the morning star declares day and night are equal.
DAUGHTER: You spoke of the Earth—is that the dark
    and heavy world lighted by the moon?
INDRA'S VOICE: Of all the spheres that wander in space,
    it is the darkest and most dense.
DAUGHTER: Doesn't the sun shine there?
INDRA'S VOICE: It shines, yes, but not always.
DAUGHTER: The clouds are parting. I can see the Earth—
INDRA'S VOICE: What do you see, child?

DAUGHTER: I see that Earth is beautiful—green forests,
blue lakes, white mountains, yellow fields.
INDRA'S VOICE: Yes, Earth is beautiful, as are all things Brahma made.
But at the dawn of time it was more beautiful still.
Then something happened,
a change of orbit, or perhaps even
a revolt that had to be quelled.
DAUGHTER: I hear sounds from below.
What race of creatures lives on Earth?
INDRA'S VOICE: Go down and see for yourself.
But never slander the Creator's children.
What you hear is their language.
DAUGHTER: It sounds as if—it isn't a cheerful sound.
INDRA'S VOICE: I know. Their mother tongue
is eternal complaint.
The race of Man
is dissatisfied and thankless.
DAUGHTER: You mustn't say that, for now
I hear cries of joy, and shots, and booms.
I see the flash of lightning, hear bells peal,
see fires kindled, and hear a thousand thousand
voices rising to heaven with thanks and praise.
(Pause.)
Your judgment of them is too stern, Father.
INDRA'S VOICE: Go down and see and hear, and then return
and tell me if their loud complaints are just.
DAUGHTER: Yes, I will go down; but you must follow.
INDRA'S VOICE: No, I cannot breath the air.
DAUGHTER: The cloud is sinking now. I'm suffocating.
It isn't air, but smoke and water.
It weighs so heavy it pulls me down, down;
even now I feel the reeling of this Earth.
Surely this third world can't be the best.
INDRA'S VOICE: The best? No. Nor the worst.
It's name is Dust, it whirls like all the others,
and therefore Man is often struck with dizziness,
caught somewhere between folly and madness.—
Be brave, my child, this is only a test.
DAUGHTER: *(Kneeling as the cloud descends.)* I'm sinking!

• • •

The background changes to a forest of giant hollyhocks: white, pink, crimson, sulfur-yellow, violet. Above them the gilt roof of a Castle is visible, on its summit the bud of a flower resembling a crown. Down below, beneath the walls of the Castle, lie heaps of straw covering stable litter. At either side of the stage are stylized representations that at once suggest interiors, façades, and landscapes. They remain stationary throughout the play. The GLAZIER and the DAUGHTER enter.

DAUGHTER: The castle is still rising out of the earth. Do you see how it's grown since last year, Father?

GLAZIER: *(To himself.)* I've never seen that castle before. And I've never heard of a castle growing. *(To the DAUGHTER, with conviction.)* But, yes, it's grown all of six feet. That's because they fertilized it. And if you look closely, you'll see it's sprouted a wing on the sunny side.

DAUGHTER: Isn't it almost time for it to bloom? Summer's already half gone.

GLAZIER: Don't you see the blossom up there?

DAUGHTER: Oh, I do, I do! *(She claps her hands.)* Father, why do flowers grow out of dirt?

GLAZIER: *(Piously.)* Because they don't like it. They're in a rush to reach the light where they bloom and die.

DAUGHTER: Who lives in the castle?

GLAZIER: I knew once, but I've forgotten.

DAUGHTER: I think there's a prisoner inside waiting for me to come and release him.

GLAZIER: Yes, but at what price?

DAUGHTER: One doesn't haggle over one's duty. Let's go in.

GLAZIER: Yes, let's.

(They go toward the rear which slowly opens to either side revealing a simple, bare room with a table and a few chairs. Seated on a chair is an OFFI-CER dressed in an unconventional modern uniform. He rocks in the chair and strikes the table with his sword. The DAUGHTER and the GLAZIER enter. The DAUGHTER approaches the OFFICER and gently takes the sword from his hand.)

DAUGHTER: You mustn't, you mustn't!

OFFICER: Please, Agnes, don't take the sword!

DAUGHTER: But you'll hack the table to bits. *(To the GLAZIER.)* Go down to the harness room and put in the window pane. We'll meet later. *(The GLAZIER goes off.)* You're a prisoner here in your own rooms. I've come to set you free.

OFFICER: I know, I've waited for this, but I was never sure you'd want to.

DAUGHTER: This is a strong castle—seven walls thick—but we'll make it out. Do you want to or not?

OFFICER: I honestly don't know. Whatever I do, I'm in trouble. Every joy is paid for with a double share of sorrow. Life is difficult here, but to buy my freedom will triple my suffering. Agnes—I'll bear with it, if only I can see you.

DAUGHTER: What do you see in me?

OFFICER: Beauty—the harmony of the universe. Your form has lines that I've found only in the movement of stars, in the beauty of sounding strings, in the vibrations of light. You're a child of heaven!

DAUGHTER: So are you!

OFFICER: Then why am I tending horses? Why am I cleaning stables and shoveling manure?

DAUGHTER: So you'll want to escape.

OFFICER: I *do* want to, but how? It's so difficult!

DAUGHTER: It's your duty to seek freedom in light.

OFFICER: Duty? Life has never done its duty by me!

DAUGHTER: Do you feel life has wronged you?

OFFICER: Yes! It's been unjust!

(Voices are heard from behind the screen that is immediately drawn aside. The OFFICER and the DAUGHTER look in that direction, their gestures and expressions frozen.—Seated at the table is the MOTHER, who is an invalid. In front of her burn candles that she trims every so often with snuffers. Piles of newly sewn undershirts lie on the table; she marks them with a quill pen and ink. Off to the left is a brown cabinet.)

FATHER: *(Has brought a silk scarf for the MOTHER and speaks in a gentle voice.)* Don't you want it?

MOTHER: A silk shawl? For me? Oh, but, my dear, what good is it, when I'm going to die soon?

FATHER: Then you believe the doctor?

MOTHER: I believe him. Yes. And I believe the voice inside me here.

FATHER: *(Sadly.)* So it's serious! And yet, all you think about is your children!

MOTHER: They were my life, my reason for being, my joy, my sorrow.

FATHER: Forgive me, Kristin. For everything.

MOTHER: But for what? You must forgive *me,* my dear. We've both plagued each other. And for what? We don't know. We couldn't do otherwise. But anyway, here's the children's new linen. Be sure they change twice a week. Wednesdays and Sundays. And see Louisa washes them—all over. Are you going out?

FATHER: I have to be at the school by eleven.

MOTHER: Would you ask Alfred to come in before you leave?

FATHER: *(Pointing to the OFFICER.)* But, my dear—he's right here.

MOTHER: Ah, my eyes are failing me, too. Yes, it's growing dark. *(Trims a candle.)* Alfred! Come! *(The FATHER goes out through the middle of the wall, nodding good-bye to the MOTHER. The OFFICER approaches the MOTHER.)* Who is the girl over there?

OFFICER: *(Whispering.)* It's Agnes!

MOTHER: Oh? Is that Agnes? Do you know what they say? They say she's the daughter of the god Indra. And that she begged to come down to earth to learn what human life is really like. But don't say a word about it!

OFFICER: She's a true child of God.

MOTHER: *(Aloud.)* Dearest Alfred, I'm going to be leaving you soon—you and your brothers and sisters. There's something I want to tell you—something you must never forget.

OFFICER: *(Sadly.)* What is it, mother?

MOTHER: Just this. You must never quarrel with God.

OFFICER: I don't understand.

MOTHER: Never go about feeling that life has wronged you.

OFFICER: But I've been treated so unjustly!

MOTHER: For stealing the coin that was found later? Is that it?

OFFICER: Yes, and that injustice has twisted my whole life!

MOTHER: I see. Go to that cabinet over there.

OFFICER: *(Ashamed.)* So you know about that, too! It's—

MOTHER: *The Swiss Family Robinson* that—

OFFICER: Don't say anymore—

MOTHER:—that your brother was punished for. Yet you were the one who tore it to bits and hid it.

OFFICER: Imagine—that cabinet still here after twenty years! And all the times we've moved! And my mother died ten years ago!

MOTHER: Well, what of it? You're always asking questions—*and* ruining the best life has to offer!—Lina's coming.

LINA: *(Enters.)* Thank you all the same, ma'am, but I can't go to the christening—

MOTHER: Why not, child?

LINA: I haven't anything to wear, ma'am.

MOTHER: Then I'll let you borrow my shawl.

LINA: Oh, no, ma'am, no, that would never do!

MOTHER: I don't understand. I won't be needing it anymore.

OFFICER: What will father say? After all, he gave it to you.

MOTHER: How petty you are.

FATHER: *(Sticking his head in.)* Lend my present to the maid?

MOTHER: Father, don't. I was a servant once myself, remember. Why hurt an innocent girl's feelings?

FATHER: And mine? I'm your husband.

MOTHER: Oh, this life! Do something good, and someone will say it's bad. Be kind to one person and you're bound to be hurting another! Ah, this life! *(She trims the candle till it goes out. The stage grows dark. The screen is brought back into place.)*

DAUGHTER: Alas for mankind!

OFFICER: Do you really think so?

DAUGHTER: Yes. Life is difficult. But love conquers all. Come and see. *(The backdrop rises to reveal a shabby, peeling wall. In the middle of it is a gate opening into a path leading to a light green plot of grass on which grows a gigantic blue monkshood or aconite. Left, in front of the gate, is a STAGE-DOOR KEEPER with a shawl over her head and shoulders, crocheting a star-spangled coverlet. To the right is a round billboard being cleaned by the BILL-POSTER. Beside him lies a fishnet with a green handle. Farther right, a door with an air hole in the shape of a four-leaf clover. Left of the gate stands a small linden tree with coal black trunk and a few light green leaves. Beside it is a manhole.)*

DAUGHTER: *(Approaching the STAGE-DOOR KEEPER.)* Isn't the coverlet finished yet?

STAGE-DOOR KEEPER: No, my dear. Twenty-six years are nothing for such a piece of work!

DAUGHTER: And your sweetheart never returned?

STAGE-DOOR KEEPER: No, but it wasn't really his fault. He *had* to go away, poor man! It's been thirty years now!

DAUGHTER: *(To the BILL-POSTER.)* Wasn't she with the ballet? Here at the opera house?

BILL-POSTER: She was the prima ballerina, the star! But when *he* left, you might say he took her dancing-feet with him. And so she got no more roles.

DAUGHTER: All they do is complain—with their eyes and their voices—

BILL-POSTER: I haven't much to complain about—not now that I've got a fishnet and a green fishbox.

DAUGHTER: And that makes you happy?

BILL-POSTER: Oh, yes! Very! It was my childhood dream. Now it's come true. Of course I'm fifty now, but—

DAUGHTER: Fifty years for a fishnet and a fishbox!

BILL-POSTER: A *green* fishbox, a *green* one—

DAUGHTER: *(To the STAGE-DOOR KEEPER.)* Give me your shawl, and I'll sit here and watch the people. But you'll have to stand behind me to explain things. *(She puts the shawl around her shoulders and sits beside the gate.)*

STAGE-DOOR KEEPER: This is the last day. The opera season's almost over. They'll soon learn if they've been signed for next year.

DAUGHTER: And those who aren't?

STAGE-DOOR KEEPER: Jesus God, you should see them! I always pull the shawl up over my head.

DAUGHTER: The poor things!

STAGE-DOOR KEEPER: Look, there's one coming now. No, she hasn't been signed. See there? She's crying.

(The SINGER hurries in from the right and goes out through the gate, her handkerchief at her eyes. She stops for a moment in the path beyond the gate and leans her head against the wall, then goes out quickly.)

DAUGHTER: Alas for mankind!

STAGE-DOOR KEEPER: Ah, but look there! There comes one who seems happy! *(The OFFICER enters through the gate. He is dressed in frock coat and top hat, and carries a bouquet of roses. He appears radiantly happy.)* He's going to marry Miss Victoria!

OFFICER: *(Downstage, looks up and sings.)* Victoria!

STAGE-DOOR KEEPER: The young lady will be out soon!

OFFICER: Excellent! The carriage is waiting, the table's set, the champagne's on ice—Ladies, I should like to embrace you! *(Embraces them, then sings out.)* Victoria!

WOMAN'S VOICE. I'm here!

OFFICER: *(Begins pacing about.)* All right! I'm waiting!

DAUGHTER: Do you know me?

OFFICER: No, I know only one woman! Victoria! For seven years I've paced back and forth here waiting for her. At noon when the sun rises high over the chimneys, and in the evening when darkness begins to fall. Look here at the pavement. The path worn by a faithful lover. Hurrah!

She's mine! *(Sings out.)* Victoria! *(There is no reply.)* I guess she must be dressing. *(To the BILL-POSTER.)* Ah, I see you've got a fishnet! Everyone at the opera is wild about fishnets! Or rather fish. Dumb fish, that is, because they can't sing. What does a thing like that cost?

BILL-POSTER: Pretty expensive!

OFFICER: *(Sings out.)* Victoria! *(Shakes the linden tree.)* Look, it's blooming again! For the eighth time. *(Sings out.)* Victoria! She must be fixing her hair. *(To the DAUGHTER.)* Ma'am, may I go up and fetch my bride?

STAGE-DOOR KEEPER: No one's allowed on stage.

OFFICER: I've paced back and forth here for seven years! Seven times three hundred and sixty-five makes two thousand five hundred and fifty-five! *(Stops and points at the door with the four-leaf clover opening.)* And I have seen this door two thousand five hundred and fifty-five times, and still I don't know where it leads! And that four-leaf clover to let in the light! Who does it let light in to?

STAGE-DOOR KEEPER: I don't know. I've never seen it open.

OFFICER: It looks like a pantry door I saw when I was four, on a Sunday visit with the maid to see her friends—other families and other maids. But I never got any farther than the kitchen and always had to sit between the water barrel and the salt tub. I've seen a lot of kitchens in my time, and the pantries are always in the passageway, with round holes and a four-leaf clover in the door. But surely there can't be a pantry at the opera because there isn't a kitchen. *(Sings out.)* Victoria! Tell me, ma'am, could she have taken another way out?

STAGE-DOOR KEEPER: There is no other way.

OFFICER: Good. Then I can't very well miss her. *(MEMBERS OF THE OPERA COMPANY swarm out. The OFFICER watches them carefully.)* She's sure to come any minute. *(To the DAUGHTER.)* Ma'am! That blue monkshood out there! I saw it when I was just a child. Is it the same one? I remember a parsonage—I was seven—and two doves—two blue doves sat there under the hood. But then a bee came along and flew into the hood. And I thought: "Now I've got you!" And I grabbed the flower and held it shut. But the bee stung me clear through the petals and I cried. The pastor's wife came then and rubbed mud on it. For supper we had wild strawberries and milk. I think it's already growing dark. *(To the BILL-POSTER.)* Where are you going?

BILL-POSTER: Home! Supper! *(Goes out.)*

OFFICER: *(Rubbing his eyes.)* Supper? At this time of day? Listen to him! *(To the DAUGHTER.)* Excuse me—may I go inside for a moment and telephone the Growing Castle?

DAUGHTER: Why?

OFFICER: To tell the Glazier to put in double windows. It's almost winter, and I freeze so easily. *(Goes in.)*

DAUGHTER: *(To the STAGE-DOOR KEEPER.)* Who is this Victoria?

STAGE-DOOR KEEPER: The woman he loves!

DAUGHTER: Right! Who she is for us or anyone else doesn't matter. It's who she is for him that counts.

(Darkness comes on quickly.)

STAGE-DOOR KEEPER: *(Lighting the lantern.)* It's growing dark early today.

DAUGHTER: To the gods a year is no more than a moment.

STAGE-DOOR KEEPER: And to mankind a moment can be longer than a year!

OFFICER: *(Reenters. He is covered with dust and the roses are wilted.)* Hasn't she come yet?

STAGE-DOOR KEEPER: No.

OFFICER: But she *will* come! She *will* come! *(Pacing back and forth.)* Still, it might be best to cancel the luncheon. Now that it's evening. Yes, yes, I'll do that. *(Goes back in to telephone.)*

STAGE-DOOR KEEPER: *(To the DAUGHTER.)* May I have my shawl back?

DAUGHTER: No, dear, I'll take your place for now. You rest. I want to learn about people and life on earth. I need to know if it's as hard as they say.

STAGE-DOOR KEEPER: There's no sleeping on this job, you know, night or day—

DAUGHTER: Not even at night?

STAGE-DOOR KEEPER: Yes, if you can manage with a bell cord tied to your arm—the night watchmen on stage are changed every three hours.

DAUGHTER: But that's torture—

STAGE-DOOR KEEPER: Think what you like. But here we're happy even to get a job like this. If only you knew how they all envy me.

DAUGHTER: Envy? The tortured are envied?

STAGE-DOOR KEEPER: Yes. But let me tell you what's even worse than the drudgery of watching all night, or the cold drafts, or dampness. It's having to listen to the troubles of all those inside. They come to me. Why? Because they read the mystery of suffering in the wrinkles of my face. It encourages them to take me into their confidence. Thirty years of torment are hidden in this shawl, my dear—mine as well as theirs.

DAUGHTER: It's heavy, and stings like nettles.

STAGE-DOOR KEEPER: Wear it if you like. And when it grows too heavy, call me. I'll relieve you.

DAUGHTER: Good-bye. I can bear as much as you.

STAGE-DOOR KEEPER: We'll see. Be good to my poor friends. Don't tire of their complaints. *(Goes out down the path.)*

(The stage grows dark. When after a moment the lights come up again the linden tree is bare, the blue monkshood almost wilted, and the green plot of grass at the end of the path brown with the color of autumn. (The OFFICER enters. He now has gray hair and a gray beard. His clothes are ragged, his collar soiled and limp. The roses he still carries have lost their petals so that only the stems remain. He paces back and forth.)

OFFICER. By all appearances summer is past and autumn almost here. I can see that by looking at the linden tree and the monkshood. *(Pacing back and forth.)* But autumn is spring to me because the theater opens again! And so she's sure to come! *(To the DAUGHTER.)* Dear lady, do you mind if I sit on this chair for a while?

DAUGHTER: Of course, my friend. I don't mind standing. *(Rises.)*

OFFICER: *(Sits down.)* If only I could sleep a bit, it would be so much better. *(Sleeps for a moment, then starts up and wanders back and forth once more. He finally stops in front of the door with the clover leaf and touches it.)* This door—won't let me rest. What's behind it? There must be something. *(Soft music in a dance rhythm is heard from above.)* Aha! They've started rehearsals! *(The stage now alternates between light and dark, as though illuminated by a lighthouse beam.)* What's this? *(Speaks in time with the flashes of light.)* Light and dark, light and dark?

DAUGHTER: *(Imitating his timing.)* Day and night, day and night! There's a merciful Providence trying to shorten your wait. And so, the days fly by, chasing the nights.

(The stage now remains light. The BILL-POSTER enters with his net and his bill-posting equipment.)

OFFICER: There's the Bill-poster with his net. Have a good catch?

BILL-POSTER: Oh, yes! It was a long, warm summer. The net was all right. But not quite what I expected.

OFFICER: *(Emphasizing his words.)* "Not quite what I expected!" Very well put. I have never yet found anything that was quite what I expected. The thought is always more than the deed, greater than the reality. *(Pacing back and forth again, striking the bouquet of roses against the walls so that the last remaining leaves and petals fall off.)*

BILL-POSTER: Hasn't she come down yet?

OFFICER: Not yet. But she'll come soon. Tell me. Do you know what's behind this door?

BILL-POSTER: No. I've never seen it open.

OFFICER: I'll telephone a locksmith to open it for us. *(Goes in to telephone.) (The BILL-POSTER posts a bill and starts out right.)*

DAUGHTER: What was wrong with your net?

BILL-POSTER: Wrong? Well, it's not that anything's wrong exactly. But it just wasn't quite what I thought it would be, so I didn't enjoy it as much.

DAUGHTER: What did you expect?

BILL-POSTER: Well, I can't say exactly.

DAUGHTER: Then let me tell you. You thought it was what it wasn't. It was supposed to be green, but not that *kind* of green.

BILL-POSTER: Yes, you do, you understand! You understand everything. And that's why everyone comes to you with their troubles. If you'd like to listen to *my* troubles, just once, I'd—

DAUGHTER: I'd be happy to. Come inside here and tell me everything. *(She goes into her room. The BILL-POSTER stands outside and talks to her through the window. The stage grows completely dark again. When the lights come up the linden tree is once more completely covered with leaves, and the monkshood is in bloom. The sun streams across the green plot at the end of the path. The OFFICER comes out. He is now old and white-haired, ragged and with torn shoes. He carries the stems of the roses and paces slowly back and forth like an old man. He reads the playbill. A BALLET GIRL enters from the right.)*

OFFICER: Has Miss Victoria left yet?

BALLET GIRL. No, she's still inside.

OFFICER: Then I'll wait. Do you think she'll come soon?

BALLET GIRL: *(Seriously.)* Oh, yes.

OFFICER: Don't go yet. You'll soon be able to see what's behind this door. I've sent for the locksmith.

BALLET GIRL: It'll be interesting to see it opened. The door *and* the Growing Castle. Do you know the Growing Castle?

OFFICER: I should hope so! I was a prisoner there!

BALLET GIRL: Really? Was that you? But why were there so many horses?

OFFICER: Because it was a stable castle.

BALLET GIRL: *(Sadly.)* How stupid of me. I should have known. *(A CHORUS GIRL enters from the right.)*

OFFICER: Has Miss Victoria left yet?

CHORUS GIRL: *(Seriously.)* No, she's still inside. She never leaves.

OFFICER: That's because she loves me. No, don't go yet. Not before the locksmith comes to open the door.

CHORUS GIRL. The door? Opened? Oh, how wonderful! I only want to ask the doorkeeper something.

(The PROMPTER enters from the right.)

OFFICER: Has Miss Victoria left yet?

PROMPTER: Not that I know of.

OFFICER: You see! What did I tell you? She's waiting for me! Don't go. The door's about to be opened.

PROMPTER: Which door?

OFFICER: Is there more than one?

PROMPTER: Oh, yes! The one with the clover leaf. I wouldn't miss it. I only want to have a word with the doorkeeper.

(The BALLET GIRL, the CHORUS GIRL, and the STAGE-DOOR KEEPER, along with the BILL-POSTER, form a group around the DOORKEEPER's window, then speak in turns to the DAUGHTER. The GLAZIER enters through the gate.)

OFFICER: Are you the locksmith?

GLAZIER: No, the locksmith is busy. Besides, a glazier's just as good.

OFFICER: Yes, of course. Of course. But do you have your diamonds with you?

GLAZIER: Naturally! What the use of a glazier without his diamonds?

OFFICER: Nothing! All right. Let's get to work.

(He claps his hands. They all assemble in a semi-circle around the door. CHORUS GIRLS dressed in costumes from Die Meistersinger, *and the BALLET GIRLS dressed in costumes from* Aïda, *enter from the right.)*

OFFICER: Locksmith—or glazier—do your duty! *(The GLAZIER steps forward with his diamond.)* Such a moment does not occur often in one lifetime. And therefore, my good friends, I beg of you to consider seriously—

POLICEMAN: *(Enters.)* In the name of the law I forbid the opening of this door!

OFFICER: Lord, the trouble when we attempt something new and glorious! Very well, we'll take it to court—get a lawyer—see what the law has to say about this!

(In full view of the audience the scene changes to the LAWYER's office. The gate remains in place and serves as the entrance to the office in a railing stretching across the entire stage. The DOORKEEPER's room has become the place for the LAWYER's desk. It is open at the front. The leafless linden tree

now becomes a hat stand. The round billboard is now hung with notices and court decisions. The door with the clover leaf is now part of the cabinet for documents. The LAWYER, in coat and white tie, sits to the left of the gate, at a desk piled high with papers. His face testifies to unheard-of sufferings. It is white as chalk and deeply furrowed with shadows that are almost violet. He is hideous. His face mirrors every kind of crime and vice with which he has to occupy himself in the daily course of his profession. Of his two CLERKS, the first has only one arm, and the other only one eye. The PEOPLE who had gathered to see the opening of the door stand there now as though to see the LAWYER. They look as if they had been standing there forever. The DAUGHTER, wearing the shawl, and the OFFICER stand in front of the others. The LAWYER goes toward the DAUGHTER.)

LAWYER: If you'll let me have the shawl, my dear, I'll hang it here. Once I've lighted the stove I'll burn it with all its sorrows and miseries.

DAUGHTER: Not yet. I want it to be full first. But most of all I want to gather up in it your *own* afflictions—the confessions you've had to hear, of crimes and vices, of thefts and slanders, libels and false arrests—

LAWYER: Your shawl, dear friend, could never do for all that. Look at these walls—the wallpaper dirtied by every sort of crime. And at these documents that hold accounts of injustice. And at me. No one ever comes here with a smile—only hard looks, bared teeth, clenched fists. And they spray their evil all over me, their envy, their suspicions. Look—my hands are black—never to come clean. Do you see how cracked they are? How bloody? My clothes can't be worn for more than a few days because they smell of other people's crimes. I often fumigate with sulfur, but it doesn't help. I sleep in the next room, and dream of nothing but crimes. I have a murder case in court right now. That's bad enough. But do you know what's worst of all? Separating husbands and wives. It's as if heaven and earth together screamed out in agony. A cry of treason against creation. Against goodness. Against love. And do you know? When papers, piled high as a mountain, are filled to overflowing with mutual accusations, if some kindly person takes one or the other of the couples aside and asks in a friendly manner the simple question: "What do you really have against your husband, or wife?" —he—or she, stands there speechless, unable to give a reason—not one. Once it had to do with a green salad; another time with just a single word. But usually it's about nothing at all. Yet the suffering, the agony! I have to bear them all. Take a good look at me. Do you really suppose I could win a woman's love with these criminal's looks? And who wants a friend who collects all the city's debts? Being human is a miserable fate.

DAUGHTER: Alas for mankind!

LAWYER: Indeed. And it's a mystery to me what people live on. They marry with an income of two thousand crowns, when in fact they need four thousand. They get themselves into debt, and of course they all make debts. And so they scrape along as best they can till they die, leaving debts behind then. And who's to pay these debts? Tell me that!

DAUGHTER: He who feeds the birds.

LAWYER: True! But if He who feeds the birds descended to His earth and witnessed the sufferings of His poor children, He just might be moved to pity—

DAUGHTER: Alas for mankind!

LAWYER: Yes, indeed! *(To the OFFICER.)* What do you want?

OFFICER: Has Miss Victoria left?

LAWYER: No. You mustn't worry. Why are you poking around my cabinet?

OFFICER: It seemed this door was so like a—

LAWYER: No, no, no!

(Church bells ring.)

OFFICER: Is there a funeral?

LAWYER: No, a commencement. Doctoral candidates are receiving their degrees. And I have to hurry. I'm about to become a Doctor of Law. Would you like to become a Doctor? Have a laurel wreath placed on your head?

OFFICER: Well, yes, why not? That's one way to kill time.

LAWYER: Excellent! Let's get ready to march in the procession! Get dressed.

(The OFFICER goes off. The stage grows dark while the scene is changed. The gate remains and serves as a chancel railing. The round billboard serves to indicate the numbers of the hymns to be sung. The linden tree is changed from a hat rack to a candelabrum. The LAWYER's desk becomes the Chancellor's pulpit. The door with the four-leaf clover now leads into the vestry. The CHORUS from Die Meistersinger *become HERALDS with scepters, and the FEMALE DANCERS carry laurel wreaths. The remainder serve as the CONGREGATION. The backdrop is removed and reveals a gigantic organ with a mirror above it, a keyboard below. Music is heard. At either side are the PROFESSORS OF THE FOUR FACULTIES: PHILOSOPHY, THEOLOGY, MEDICINE, and LAW. The stage is silent for a moment. The HERALDS enter from the right. They are followed by the DANCERS with laurel wreaths in their extended hands. THREE DOCTORAL*

CANDIDATES enter from the left, one after the other, are crowned by the DANCERS, and then go off right. The LAWYER steps forward to be crowned. The DANCERS turn from him, refusing to crown him, and go off. Everyone disappears. The LAWYER is left alone. The DAUGHTER enters, a white shawl over her head and shoulders.)

DAUGHTER: Look, I've just washed the shawl! But what are you doing here? Did you get the wreath?

LAWYER: I wasn't worthy.

DAUGHTER: Why? Because you defended the poor, put in a good word for the criminal, lightened the burden of the guilty, got a reprieve for the condemned? Poor mankind! They're not angels, but they're surely to be pitied.

LAWYER: Don't judge them too harshly. I have to defend them.

DAUGHTER: *(Leaning against the organ.)* Why do they slap their own friends in the face?

LAWYER: They don't know any better.

DAUGHTER: Then let's teach them. Shall we? We'll do it together.

LAWYER: They won't let themselves be taught. If only the gods in heaven would hear our cries!

DAUGHTER: Don't worry. They'll reach the throne. *(Stands beside the organ.)* Do you know what I see in this mirror? The world. But as it should be. For it's upside down as it is.

LAWYER: How did it get that way?

DAUGHTER: When the copy was made—

LAWYER: You see! There! The copy! I've always had the feeling it was a copy—a bad copy! And when I began to recall the original, I became dissatisfied with everything. They said I was cynical and had a jaundiced eye, and on and on—

DAUGHTER: It's an insane world! Look at the four faculties. Each supported by the same civil government. Theology, the doctrine about God, is constantly attacked and ridiculed by philosophy, which claims it alone has wisdom. And medicine, always discounting theology as one of the sciences, calls it superstition. And they sit together in the council meant to teach the young respect for the university! Why, it's a madhouse! I pity the first man who comes to his senses!

LAWYER: The first to discover this are the theologians. They start off by studying philosophy that tells them that theology is nonsense, and then they read in their theology that philosophy is nonsense. And all of it nothing but madness.

DAUGHTER: And the law that serves everyone but its own servants!

LAWYER: And justice that destroys the just in trying to be just! Justice that is so often unjust!

DAUGHTER: And it's all your doing, children of man.—Come, child. I'll give you a crown more fitting. *(Places a crown of thorns on his head.)* And now I'll pray for you. *(Sits at the organ and plays a Kyrie, but instead of the organ we hear the singing of human voices.)*

CHILDREN'S VOICES: Lord! Lord! *(The last chord is held.)*

WOMEN'S VOICES: Have mercy on us! *(The last chord is held.)*

MEN'S VOICES: *(Tenor.)* Deliver us for Thy sweet mercy's sake! *(The last chord is held.)*

MEN'S VOICES: *(Bass.)* Save Thy children, O Lord, and turn Thine anger from us!

ALL: Have mercy on us! Hear us! Turn Your compassion upon us!—Lord, why hast Thou forsaken us? Out of the depths, O Lord, we cry to Thee! Have mercy! Make not Thy children's burden too great! Hear us! Hear us! *(The stage grows dark. The DAUGHTER rises and goes to the LAWYER. A change in lighting transforms the organ into Fingal's Cave. The sea surges in under the basalt columns. The wind and the waves combine in a great harmonious sound.)*

LAWYER: Where are we, sister?

DAUGHTER: What do you hear?

LAWYER: Drops falling—

DAUGHTER: The tears of mankind weeping. What else do you hear?

LAWYER: Sighing—moaning—wailing—

DAUGHTER: Man's cries reach this far, no farther. But why this eternal lament? Is there no joy in life?

LAWYER: Yes—the sweetest that is also the bitterest. Love! Marriage and a home! The highest and the lowest!

DAUGHTER: I have to try!

LAWYER: With me?

DAUGHTER: With you! You know the rocks and dangerous places. We'll avoid them.

LAWYER: But I'm poor.

DAUGHTER: Does that matter, as long as we love each other? A little beauty costs nothing.

LAWYER: I hate things that you might love.

DAUGHTER: Then we'll compromise.

LAWYER: And when we grow tired of each other?

DAUGHTER: We'll have a child who will bring us happiness that will never grow old.

LAWYER: You'll take me as I am? Poor, ugly, despised, rejected?

DAUGHTER: Yes! We'll join our destinies!

LAWYER: So be it!

• • •

A very simple room beside the LAWYER's office. At the right is a large bed with a canopy; beside it a window. To the left is an iron stove with cooking utensils. KRISTIN is busy applying strips of paper along the joints of the inner window. A glass door in the background leads into the office; behind it we see a number of poorly dressed PEOPLE waiting to be admitted.

KRISTIN. I'm pasting, I'm pasting!

DAUGHTER: *(Pale and worn, sitting at the stove.)* You're shutting out the air! I'm suffocating—

KRISTIN. There's only a small crack left.

DAUGHTER: Air, air! I can't breathe!

KRISTIN. I'm pasting, I'm pasting!

LAWYER: That's right, Kristin! Heat is costly!

DAUGHTER: It's as if you were pasting my mouth shut!

LAWYER: *(In the doorway, a document in his hand.)* Is the baby sleeping?

DAUGHTER: Yes, finally!

LAWYER: *(Softly.)* His screaming drives my clients away.

DAUGHTER: *(Gently.)* What can we do about it?

LAWYER: Nothing.

DAUGHTER: We'll have to find a larger apartment.

LAWYER: We haven't any money.

DAUGHTER: May I open the window? The air in here is making me choke.

LAWYER: The heat will escape and we'll freeze.

DAUGHTER: It's horrible! Can't we at least scrub the floor out there?

LAWYER: You aren't strong enough, and neither am I. And Kristin has to go on pasting. She has to paste the whole house shut. Every crack in the floor, the walls, the ceiling.

DAUGHTER: I was prepared for poverty, not for dirt.

LAWYER: Poverty is always relatively dirty.

DAUGHTER: It's worse than I ever dreamed.

LAWYER: It could be worse. There's still food in the pot.

DAUGHTER: You call that food?

LAWYER: Cabbage is cheap, nourishing, and good.

DAUGHTER: If you like cabbage. I can't stand it.

LAWYER: Why didn't you say so?

DAUGHTER: Because I loved you. I wanted to sacrifice for you.

LAWYER: Then I'll have to sacrifice my love for cabbage. Sacrifices must be mutual.

DAUGHTER: Then what will we eat? Fish? You hate fish.

LAWYER: It's also expensive.

DAUGHTER: Life is harder than I ever dreamed.

LAWYER: *(Gently.)* Yes, now you see how hard it is. And the child who was to have been our bond and blessing has become our ruin.

DAUGHTER: Oh, my dear! I'm dying in this air, in this room with its view of the yard, and the child's endless screaming, keeping me awake, and those people out there with their wailing and quarreling and accusations! I'll die in this room!

LAWYER: Poor little flower! Without light, without air—

DAUGHTER: And you say there are those who are worse off—

LAWYER: I'm one of the most envied men in the neighborhood.

DAUGHTER: I could bear it if only I had some beauty in here.

LAWYER: I know—I know what you mean—a flower—a heliotrope especially. But that costs one and a half—that's six bottles of milk or half a bushel of potatoes.

DAUGHTER: I'd gladly do without food if only I had my flower.

LAWYER: There's a kind of beauty that costs nothing. Not to have it is the worst torture for a man with any sense of beauty.

DAUGHTER: And what's that?

LAWYER: No, you'll get angry.

DAUGHTER: We agreed never to be angry.

LAWYER: We agreed—yes—I know. Everything will be all right, Agnes, if only there are no hard words. Do you know what I mean? No, not yet!

DAUGHTER: And there never will be.

LAWYER: Never, as long as it depends on me.

DAUGHTER: Go on.

LAWYER: Well—whenever I go into a house the first thing I notice is how the curtains are hanging. *(He goes to the curtains at the window and puts them in order.)* And if they're hanging crooked and look like rags—I leave. And then I look at the chairs. If they're in their proper places, I stay. *(He pushes a chair to the wall.)* Then I look at the candles in their holders. If they're crooked, the whole house is a mess. *(He straightens the candles on the sideboard.)* And so you see, my dear, there's the beauty that costs nothing.

DAUGHTER: *(Drops her head.)* Those are hard words, Axel!

LAWYER: They're not!

DAUGHTER: They *are!*

LAWYER: The hell with it!

DAUGHTER: What kind of language is that?

LAWYER: I'm sorry, Agnes. But I've suffered as much from your slovenliness as you have from the dirt. And I didn't dare put things straight for fear you'd get mad and think I was scolding you. Ugh! Shall we stop this now?

DAUGHTER: Why is marriage so hard? Can there be anything harder? One has to be an angel to survive.

LAWYER: I know.

DAUGHTER: I think I'm beginning to hate you!

LAWYER: Then I pity us. But let's keep hatred out of it. I promise you, Agnes, I'll never complain of your housekeeping again, no matter if it tortures me.

DAUGHTER: And I'll eat cabbage, no matter if it tortures me.

LAWYER: A life together in agony, then. One's pleasure, the other's pain!

DAUGHTER: Alas for mankind!

LAWYER: You understand that now?

DAUGHTER: Yes. But in God's name let's avoid the rocks. We know them so well by now.

LAWYER: Yes. All right. We'll do that. After all, we're humane, enlightened people. We can forgive and forget.

DAUGHTER: We can even smile at trifles.

LAWYER: We can. Yes, we can.—You know, I read in the paper this morning—by the way, where is the paper?

DAUGHTER: *(Embarrassed.)* Which paper?

LAWYER: *(Harshly.)* Do I take more than one paper?

DAUGHTER: Smile—don't be so hard.—I used it to light the fire this morning.

LAWYER: *(Violently.)* The hell you did!

DAUGHTER: Smile!—I burned it because it ridiculed what is sacred to me.

LAWYER: And what is *not* sacred to *me!* Hm! *(Slams his fist into his other hand furiously.)* I'll smile! I'll smile till my molars show! I'll be considerate, I'll hide my thoughts, I'll say yes to everything, I'll evade it all and play the hypocrite! All right, so you've burned the paper. Well, well— *(Straightens the curtains at the bed.)* There, I'm straightening up again, and you'll lose your temper. Oh, Agnes, this is impossible!

DAUGHTER: I know, I know—

LAWYER: But we'll go on, not because of our vows, but for the child.

DAUGHTER: Yes. For the child.—We *must* go on, we *must*—

LAWYER: I have to get back to my clients. Listen to them. Mumbling with impatience. Can't wait to tear one another to pieces, get each other fined and thrown into prison—lost souls—

DAUGHTER: Poor unhappy people. And this pasting! *(Lowers her head in silent despair.)*

KRISTIN. I'm pasting, I'm pasting!

(The LAWYER stands at the door, nervously fingering the handle.)

DAUGHTER: Oh, the squeal of that doorknob! It's like you were twisting my heart in your fist—

LAWYER: I'm twisting, I'm twisting—

DAUGHTER: Don't!

LAWYER: I'm twisting—

DAUGHTER: No!

LAWYER: I—

OFFICER: *(Enters from the office, taking hold of the door handle.)* May I intrude?

LAWYER: *(Lets loose of the handle.)* Of course! Since you have your degree now!

OFFICER: And all the world is mine! All paths open to me! Parnassus scaled, laurels won, immortality and fame! Everything, mine!

LAWYER: How will you live?

OFFICER: Live?

LAWYER: You'll need a roof over your head, clothes, food?

OFFICER: No problem when there's someone who loves you.

LAWYER: Imagine that! Imagine!—Paste, Kristin, paste! Till they can't breathe. *(Goes out backwards, nodding.)*

KRISTIN. I'm pasting, I'm pasting! Till they can't breathe!

OFFICER: Will you come with me now?

DAUGHTER: Yes! Now! But where?

OFFICER: To Fairhaven. It's summer there, the sun's shining, youth and children and flowers! Singing, dancing, feasting, rejoicing!

DAUGHTER: I want to go there!

OFFICER: Come!

LAWYER: *(Reenters.)* I'll go back to my first hell. This was the second, and the greatest. The most beautiful hell is always the greatest.—Look at this, she's left hairpins lying on the floor again. *(Picks one up.)*

OFFICER: Good Lord, he's found the hairpins, too.

LAWYER: Too? Look at this one. Two prongs, but one pin. Two and yet one. Straighten it and it becomes one. Bend it again and it's two, without ever ceasing to be one. That is to say, two are one! And yet if I break it—like this—then the two are two. *(Breaks the hairpin and throws the pieces away.)*

OFFICER: So he understands it all!—But before you can break it, the two prongs must diverge. If they converge, then it holds.

LAWYER: And if they're parallel—they'll never meet. It neither holds nor breaks.

OFFICER: The hairpin! The most perfect of created objects! A straight line which at the same time is two parallels!

LAWYER: A lock that closes when it's open!

OFFICER: Like this door. In closing it I open the way for you, Agnes. *(Goes out and closes the door.)*

DAUGHTER: And now?

(The scene changes. The bed with the curtains becomes a tent. The iron stove remains. The backdrop is raised. Downstage right is a burned hillside with red heather and black-and-white tree stumps left by a forest fire, along with red pigsties and farmhouses. Below it is an open-air gymnasium for remedial exercises, where people are being treated on various machines resembling instruments of torture. Downstage left is the Quarantine Station: open sheds with ovens, walled-in burners and pipes. Center stage is occupied by a narrow strait. Upstage we see a beautifully wooded shore, with piers decorated with flags. White boats are moored to them, some with sails hoisted, some without. Among the trees on the shore are small Italian villas, pavilions, kiosks, and marble statues. The QUARANTINE MASTER, dressed as a blackamoor, walks on the beach. The OFFICER goes toward him and shakes his hand.)

OFFICER: So you're here, too, you old windbag!

QUARANTINE MASTER: Indeed I am.

OFFICER: Is this Fairhaven?

QUARANTINE MASTER: No, Fairhaven is over there. *(Points.)* This is Foulstrand.

OFFICER: Then we must have taken the wrong way.

QUARANTINE MASTER: We? Won't you introduce me?

OFFICER: I'm afraid that wouldn't be proper. *(In a low voice.)* This is the Daughter of Indra.

QUARANTINE MASTER: Indra's Daughter? I thought it was Varuna herself! Well? Are you surprised to see me in blackface?

OFFICER: My dear boy, I'm fifty now and past the age of surprises. I assumed you were going to an afternoon masquerade.

QUARANTINE MASTER: Right you are! And I hope you'll join me.

OFFICER: Might as well, there's nothing much doing here. What sort of people live in this place?

QUARANTINE MASTER: The sick. The healthy ones live over there.

OFFICER: Then it must be the poor who live here.

QUARANTINE MASTER: No, not at all, my boy—the wealthy! Look at that man on the rack there. He ate too much *pâté de foie gras* with truffles and drank too much Burgundy; that's why his feet became knotted.

OFFICER: Knotted?

QUARANTINE MASTER: Yes.—And that one there, lying on the guillotine, drank so much brandy his backbone has to be rolled straight!

OFFICER: That can't be much fun either!

QUARANTINE MASTER: Everyone living here has some misery to hide. The one coming along, for example.

(An elderly DANDY is rolled along in a wheelchair, accompanied by a lean, ugly, sixty-year-old COQUETTE dressed in the latest fashion. They are in the company of a forty-year-old MALE FRIEND of hers.)

OFFICER: Why, that's the Major! Our schoolfriend!

QUARANTINE MASTER: Don Juan is more like it! As you can see, he's still in love with the scarecrow at his side. He's blind to the fact that she's old, ugly, unfaithful, and cruel.

OFFICER: That's love for you! Who'd ever have thought the lecher could love so deeply and seriously!

QUARANTINE MASTER: That's most charitable of you.

OFFICER: Well, I've been in love, too. Victoria! I still walk the corridor waiting for her—

QUARANTINE MASTER: Ah, so that's *you* in the corridor!

OFFICER: That's me, all right.

QUARANTINE MASTER: Did you ever get that door open?

OFFICER: No, it's still in litigation. The Bill-poster's on vacation just now, with his net, of course, so the testimony's been delayed. Meanwhile the Glazier has put panes in the windows of the Castle—it's grown half a story by now. It was an unusually good year. Warm and damp.

QUARANTINE MASTER: Not as warm as where I work.

OFFICER: How hot do you keep your ovens?

QUARANTINE MASTER: We disinfect possible cholera patients at one hundred and forty degrees.

OFFICER: There's a cholera epidemic?

QUARANTINE MASTER: You didn't know?

OFFICER: Well, yes, but I often forget what I know.

QUARANTINE MASTER: I often wish I *could* forget—myself especially. That's why I go to masquerades, dress balls, and amateur theatricals.

OFFICER: Why? What did you do?

QUARANTINE MASTER: When I tell, I'm a braggart, and when I don't, I'm a hypocrite.

OFFICER: Does that explain the blackface?

QUARANTINE MASTER: Yes—just a shade blacker than I am.

OFFICER: Who's that coming?

QUARANTINE MASTER: He's a poet. On the way to his mudbath.

(The POET enters, looking up at the sky, a pail of mud in his hand.)

OFFICER: From the look of him, he needs light and air!

QUARANTINE MASTER: His head's in the clouds so often he gets homesick for mud. Hardens the skin. The same with pigs. The gadflies don't sting so much then.

OFFICER: What a strange world of contradictions!

POET: *(Ecstatically.)* Out of clay the God Ptah created man on a potter's wheel, a lathe— *(Skeptically.)* —or on some other damned contraption! *(Ecstatically.)* Out of clay the sculptor fashions his more or less immortal masterpieces— *(Skeptically.)* —which for the most part are pure crap! *(Ecstatically.)* Out of clay are formed these oh-so-necessary objects for the kitchen commonly called pots and pans— *(Skeptically.)* —not that I give a damn what they're called! *(Ecstatically.)* And such is clay! When mixed with water, they call it mud. *C'est mon affaire! (Calls.)* Lina! *(LINA enters carrying a bucket.)* Lina, let Agnes have a look at you. She knew you ten years ago when you were young, happy, and, let me add, a beautiful girl. *(To the DAUGHTER.)* But look at her now! Five children, drudgery, screaming, hunger, beatings! Her beauty gone, her joy vanished—and all in the fulfillment of a duty—the duty that was to give her inner peace, and to find expression in the harmonious lines of her face, the tranquil glow of her eyes—

QUARANTINE MASTER: *(His hand covering the POET's mouth.)* Shut your hole! Shut your hole!

POET: That's what they all say. And once you've shut it, they want you to speak! Idiots! Idiots! No rhyme, no reason!

DAUGHTER: *(Going to LINA.)* Tell me your complaints?

LINA: I wouldn't dare! They'd only make it worse!

DAUGHTER: Who would be so cruel?

LINA: I don't dare—they'll beat me!

POET: That's the truth! But I'll tell even if this blackamoor knocks my teeth down my throat! Let me tell you, Agnes, Daughter of God, that injustice most certainly exists! Do you hear the music and dancing from up there on the hill? Well! It's for Lina's sister who's just returned from the city—where, let me say, she wasn't a very good girl. But now she's back, and they're slaying the fatted calf, while Lina, who stayed at home, gets to lug this bucket and feed the pigs!

DAUGHTER: There is rejoicing because the prodigal has abandoned her evil ways, and not merely because she has come home. Remember that!

POET: Fine! Then let them throw a supper and dance every evening for the innocent servant who's *never* gone astray! Do that! But they won't! For whenever Lina's free, she has to go to prayer meetings where she's preached at for not being perfect. Is that what you call justice?

DAUGHTER: Your questions are so hard to answer because—because of all the unknowns—

POET: That's exactly how the Caliph, Harun the Just, saw it. Sitting quietly on his throne, he never saw what went on down here below. Finally their complaints reached his exalted ear, and one fine day he climbed down from his throne, disguised himself, and mingled among the people unrecognized, to learn how justice had failed.

DAUGHTER: Surely you can't think I'm Harun the Just.

OFFICER: Let's talk about something else.—Look, visitors!

(A white boat in the shape of a dragon glides into the strait. It has a light blue silk sail and a golden yardarm with a rose-red pennant. Seated at the helm, their arms around each other, are HE and SHE.)

OFFICER: Look at that—perfect happiness, immeasurable bliss, and the ecstasy of young love!

(The light grows brighter. HE rises in the boat and sings.)

HE: Hail to thee, lovely bay,
   where I first knew spring,
   where I first dreamt love's golden dreams!
   You have me again,
   but not alone now!
   Forests and coves,
   heaven and sea,

greet her now!

My love, my bride!

My sun, my life!

(The flags on Fairhaven Landing dip in salute, and white handkerchiefs wave from the villas and the shore, while a chord of music from harps and violins sounds across the water.)

POET: Behold the world made light by love! And the music hovering on the waters!—Eros!

OFFICER: It's Victoria!

QUARANTINE MASTER: And what if it is?

OFFICER: Only it's *his* Victoria. I have mine all to myself, and no one will ever see her. Hoist the quarantine flag while I haul in the net! *(The QUARANTINE MASTER waves a yellow flag. The OFFICER pulls on a line causing the boat to approach Foulstrand.)* Hold it there!

(HE and SHE set foot on land and register their disgust.)

HE: What have we done?

QUARANTINE MASTER: No need to do anything to taste of life's petty discomforts.

SHE: How can joy and happiness be so brief?

HE: How long must we stay?

QUARANTINE MASTER: Forty days and nights.

SHE: We'd rather die!

HE: Live here, among charred hillsides and pigsties?

POET: Love conquers all, even sulfur and carbolic acid.

(The QUARANTINE MASTER lights an oven; blue sulfurous vapors rise up.)

QUARANTINE MASTER: I've lighted the sulfur. Step inside, please.

SHE: My blue dress will lose its color!

QUARANTINE MASTER: Yes, and turn white. Along with your roses.

HE: As well as your cheeks! In forty days!

SHE: *(To the OFFICER.)* That will please *you!*

OFFICER: No, that's not true. I admit your happiness caused my misery, but—that doesn't matter. I have my degree, and a position over there. *(Points to Fairhaven.)* Yes, indeed! And in the fall I'll have a job in a school teaching boys the same lessons I learned in my youth—the same lessons that now I'll learn all through the years of my maturity, and finally into old age. Always the same lessons. How much two times two is. How many times two goes into four. Until finally I'm pensioned off and have nothing to do but wait for mealtimes and the newspapers. And then be hauled off to the crematorium and be burned to ashes.—Don't you have any pensioners here? Surely there's nothing worse than being a pensioner. Especially after two times two is four. Beginning school all over again when you already have your degree. Asking the same questions until you die—*(An elderly man, the PENSIONER, goes past, hands behind his back.)* You see? There goes a pensioner now, just waiting for death to arrive. He's obviously a captain who never made major. Or a court clerk who was never promoted. Many are called, but few are chosen. So he walks around waiting for his breakfast.

PENSIONER. No, for the paper! The morning paper!

OFFICER: And he's only fifty-four. He could last another twenty-five years, waiting for his mealtimes and his papers. That's a horrible thought!

PENSIONER. Tell me something that isn't horrible. Tell me! Tell me!

OFFICER: Let him who *can* tell us that! *(The PENSIONER goes off.)* And now I'll go study with little boys that two times two is four. How many times two goes into four—*(Clasps his head in despair.)* And Victoria, whom I loved, for whom I wished the greatest happiness on earth—she has that happiness now, the greatest happiness she can ever know. And that's why I suffer, suffer, suffer!

SHE: Do you think I can be happy watching you suffer? How can you think that? But maybe it's a comfort to you to know that I have to sit here for forty days and nights. Is it?

OFFICER: Yes and no. How can I be happy when you suffer?

HE: And do you think I can build my happiness on your pain?

OFFICER: All of us—we're all to be pitied.

(They lift their hands to heaven and emit cries of anguish which together sound like a great dissonant chord.)

DAUGHTER: Lord, hear them! Life is an evil! Alas for mankind!

(All cry out as before.—For a moment the stage grows completely black, during which everyone either exits or changes places. When the lights come on again, Foulstrand can be seen upstage in shadow. Center stage is the water. Downstage is Fairhaven, bathed in light. To the right is a corner of the casino. The windows are open and dancing couples are seen inside. THREE GIRLS stand outside on an empty box, their arms wrapped around one another's waists as they watch the dance. On the terrace is a bench on which UGLY EDITH sits sadly, without a hat and with long disheveled hair. In front of her is an open piano, and to the left a yellow wooden house. Outside, two CHILDREN dressed in summer clothes are playing ball. In the foreground, near the strait, is a dock with white boats and flagpoles with flags waving. Farther out on the strait a white warship, a brig with gunports, is

anchored. The entire landscape appears in winter dress; snow lies upon bare trees and on the ground. The DAUGHTER and the OFFICER enter.)

DAUGHTER: There's peace and happiness here in this holiday resort. Nobody works. Parties every day. People dressed in holiday clothes. Even music and dancing before noon. *(To the THREE GIRLS.)* Children, why aren't you in there dancing?

MAID: Us?

OFFICER: But they're servants!

DAUGHTER: That's true. But why is Edith sitting here instead of dancing? *(EDITH hides her face in her hands.)*

OFFICER: Don't ask her! She's sat there for three whole hours and not a soul asked her to dance. *(He goes into the yellow house to the left.)*

DAUGHTER: What cruel pleasure!

EDITH'S MOTHER: *(Enters in a low-cut dress and goes to EDITH.)* Why don't you go on in, like I told you?

EDITH. Because—because I can't dance with myself. I know I'm ugly, and that's why no one will dance with me, but I wish you'd stop reminding me! *(She begins to play Bach's Toccata and Fugue No. 10 on the piano. The waltz, heard very faintly at first from inside the hall, grows louder as though to compete with the Bach Toccata. But EDITH's playing overcomes and silences it. The DANCERS appear at the door and listen to her in rapt silence as she plays.)*

A NAVAL OFFICER: *(Takes ALICE, one of the girls at the ball, by the waist and leads her down to the dock.)* Come on! Hurry!

(EDITH breaks off suddenly, stands, and looks after them in despair. She remains standing there as if turned to stone. The wall of the yellow house is drawn aside. Three school benches come into view with SCHOOLBOYS sitting on them. The OFFICER is among them, looking restless and worried. A bespectacled SCHOOLMASTER stands in front of them holding chalk and a cane.)

SCHOOLMASTER: *(To the OFFICER.)* Now, my boy, can you tell how much two times two is? *(The OFFICER remains seated, trying painfully to remember, but fails to find the answer.)* You are to stand when you are asked a question!

OFFICER: *(Rises, depressed.)* Two—times two—just a minute—makes two—twos.

SCHOOLMASTER: Hm! I see you haven't studied your lesson!

OFFICER: *(Embarrassed.)* No, I did, I learned it, but—I know it but I just can't say it.

SCHOOLMASTER: You're making excuses! You know it but can't say it! Perhaps I can be of some help. *(He pulls the OFFICER's hair.)*

OFFICER: This is terrible! Terrible!

SCHOOLMASTER: Yes, terrible that a big boy like you has no ambition!

OFFICER: *(Humiliated.)* Big boy! Yes, I'm big, bigger than these others! I'm a grown man! I've finished school—*(As though awakening.)* Why—why, I even have my degree!—Then why am I sitting here? Wasn't I awarded a degree?

SCHOOLMASTER: Certainly! Of course! But you still must sit here and mature, mustn't you? You must mature. Is that or is that not correct?

OFFICER: *(Hand at his forehead.)* Of course that's right. One must mature. Two times two—is two. And I can prove that by analogy, the highest form of proof! Listen!—One times one is one, therefore two times two is two. For what applies to one must apply to the other!

SCHOOLMASTER: According to the rules of logic your proof is quite correct, but the answer is wrong!

OFFICER: What is right according to the rules of logic *cannot* be wrong! Let's prove it. One goes into one one time, therefore two goes into two two times.

SCHOOLMASTER: Correct—according to the rules of analogy. But then how much is one times three?

OFFICER: Three!

SCHOOLMASTER: Consequently two times three is also three.

OFFICER: *(Considering.)* No, that can't be right—or is it? *(Sits down in despair.)* No, I'm not mature yet.

SCHOOLMASTER: No, not by a long shot—

OFFICER: But how long do I have to sit here?

SCHOOLMASTER: How long? Do you believe in time and space?—Well, assuming that time exists, you must be able to tell me what time is. What is time?

OFFICER: Time? *(Reflects.)* I can't say it, but I know. And therefore I can also know how much two times two is without being able to say it! Can *you* tell me what time is?

SCHOOLMASTER: Certainly!

SCHOOLBOYS: Then tell us!

SCHOOLMASTER: Time—let me see—*(Stands there unmoving, finger aside his nose.)* While we're talking, time runs on. Therefore time is something that runs on while I talk.

A SCHOOLBOY: *(Gets up.)* Since you're talking, sir, and while you're talking, I run, I must be time. *(And he runs on out.)*

SCHOOLMASTER: According to the rules of logic that is quite correct.

OFFICER: But then the rules of logic are insane, because Nils, who fled, can't be time.

SCHOOLMASTER: That, too, is quite correct according to the rules of logic, even though it's insane.

OFFICER: Then logic is insane.

SCHOOLMASTER: It would certainly seem so. But if logic is insane, then the whole world is insane, and why in hell should I sit here teaching you insanities! How about it! If anyone wants to treat us to a drink, we'll go for a swim!

OFFICER: That's a *posterus prius*, the world turned backward! The custom is first to have a swim and *then* a drink! You old idiot!

SCHOOLMASTER: You needn't be so conceited, Doctor!

OFFICER: Colonel, if you please! I am an officer, and I fail to understand why I sit here being scolded among schoolboys!

SCHOOLMASTER: *(Raises his finger.)* We must mature!

QUARANTINE MASTER: *(Enters.)* The quarantine's beginning!

OFFICER: Oh, there you are! Imagine, this fellow making me sit here on a school bench, and I have my degree!

QUARANTINE MASTER: Then leave, why don't you?

OFFICER: Do you mean that? Leave? That's not as simple as it sounds.

QUARANTINE MASTER: I know. But try.

OFFICER: *(To the QUARANTINE MASTER.)* Save me! Save me from his eyes!

QUARANTINE MASTER: Come along. Come to our dance. We have to dance before the plague breaks out. We do!

OFFICER: Will the ship sail then?

QUARANTINE MASTER: The ship will sail first. And that will cause many tears.

OFFICER: Tears, always tears—when it comes and when it goes! Let's go.
(They go off. The SCHOOLMASTER continues his instruction. The THREE GIRLS who were standing at the window of the hall now go sadly toward the dock. EDITH, who stood stonelike by the piano, follows them.)

DAUGHTER: *(To the OFFICER.)* Are there no happy people in this Paradise?

OFFICER: Of course. The two newlyweds over there. Just listen to them.
(The NEWLYWEDS enter.)

HUSBAND: *(To the WIFE.)* I'm so happy, I wish I could die!

WIFE: But why die?

HUSBAND: Because no happiness is without its seed of unhappiness. It consumes itself in its own flame. It can't burn forever, so it has to die. And knowing what's to come destroys my love when it burns most brightly.

WIFE: Then let's die together—now.

HUSBAND: Die! Yes! I'm afraid of happiness—happiness only betrays.

(They go toward the sea.)

DAUGHTER: *(To the OFFICER.)* Life is evil! Alas for mankind!

OFFICER: Look, do you see that man? He's the most envied of anyone here! *(The BLIND MAN is led in.)* These hundred Italian villas belong to him. These fjords and bays, these shores and forests; the fish in the water, the birds in the air, the wildlife in the woods—all are his. Everyone here is his tenant, and the sun rises over his sea and sets over his lands—

DAUGHTER: And he also complains?

OFFICER: Yes, and he has every reason too. He can't see.

QUARANTINE MASTER: He's blind.

DAUGHTER: The most envied of all!

OFFICER: He's off to the ship now—to see his son sail.

BLIND MAN: I don't see, but I hear. I hear the anchor tearing up the clay bed like a hook pulled from the throat of a fish so its heart comes up along with it. My son, my only child, is about to start a sea journey to foreign lands. I go with him only in my thoughts. I hear the chain clanking now. And there's something fluttering and flapping like wet wash on the line. Handkerchiefs damp with tears perhaps. And I hear sobbing and sighing, like people crying. Or is it waves washing against the ship— or the girls on shore—abandoned—inconsolable? I asked a child once why the sea is salty, and the child, whose father was off on a long voyage, answered at once. "The sea is salty because sailors cry so much." But why do sailors cry so much? I asked. "Well," he answered, "because they're always going away—and that's why they always dry their handkerchiefs on the mast!" Why do people cry when they're sad? I asked him. "Oh," said the child, "because the windows of their eyes have to be washed from time to time so they can see more clearly."

(The ship has hoisted sail and glides off. The GIRLS on shore wave with their handkerchiefs and alternately dry their tears. Now the signal-flag for "Yes" is hoisted to the topmast: a red sphere on a white background. ALICE waves joyfully in reply.)

DAUGHTER: *(To the OFFICER.)* What does the flag mean?

OFFICER: It means "Yes." The lieutenant gives us his "Yes" in red, red as heart's blood painted on the blue cloth of the sky.

DAUGHTER: What does "No" look like?

OFFICER: As blue as the bad blood in his veins. But look how happy Alice is.

DAUGHTER: And how Edith is crying.

BLIND MAN: Meeting and parting. Parting and meeting. Such is life. I met his mother. Then she went away. I still had my son. But now he's gone, too.

DAUGHTER: He'll be back.

BLIND MAN: Who's that talking? I've heard that voice before, in dreams, in my youth, at the start of summer vacation, when I was newly married and my child was born. Whenever life smiled at me I heard that voice, like the soughing of the south wind, like the sound of a harp above, like I imagine the angels' greeting on that Christmas Night. *(The LAWYER enters, goes to the BLIND MAN, and whispers something to him.)* Really!

LAWYER: That's how it is. *(Goes to the DAUGHTER.)* You've seen almost everything now, except for the worst.

DAUGHTER: And that is—?

LAWYER: Repetitions! Reiterations! Turning back! Redoing lessons.— Come!

DAUGHTER: Where?

LAWYER: To your duties!

DAUGHTER: Which are—?

LAWYER: Everything you despise! Everything you don't want to do but must! Abstinence, renunciation, deprivation, resignation. Everything unpleasant, repulsive, tortuous!

DAUGHTER: Aren't there any pleasant duties?

LAWYER: Only when they're behind you.

DAUGHTER: When they no longer exist—then duty is everything unpleasant! What is pleasant, then?

LAWYER: Sin.

DAUGHTER: Sin?

LAWYER: Which must be punished. If I've had a pleasant day and evening, the next day I'm plagued with the pangs of hell and a bad conscience.

DAUGHTER: How strange!

LAWYER: Yes, I wake in the morning with a headache, and then the repetition begins; but no normal repetition. Everything that the evening before had seemed beautiful, pleasant, and charming, now, in the light of day, appears ugly, repulsive, and stupid. Pleasure rots and joy falls apart. What people call success is only the beginning of the next failure; my successes have been my undoing. Humans have an innate horror of other people's success; they feel it's unjust that fate should favor any one person, and so they try to restore the balance by rolling stones in their path. Talent is a dangerous thing—you can starve to death! Go back to your duties now, or I'll have to sue you, and we'll go through all three courts, one, two, three.

DAUGHTER: Back? To that iron stove and the pot of cabbage and the baby's clothes?

LAWYER: Yes. Today's wash day. We'll be washing all the handkerchiefs.

DAUGHTER: Do I have to—all over again?

LAWYER: Life is constant repetition. Look at the schoolmaster in there. He got his doctorate yesterday, was crowned with laurel to the sound of cannons, ascended Parnassus, was embraced by the king—and today he starts school all over again, asking how much two times two is, and will do that till the day he dies. But come back to your home now.

DAUGHTER: I'd rather die!

LAWYER: Die? It's not allowed! First, because it's dishonorable—so dishonorable that even your corpse is disgraced; and second, you're damned—it's a mortal sin!

DAUGHTER: It isn't easy being human!

ALL: Yes!

DAUGHTER: No, I won't go back with you! Not to that dirt and degradation! I'll go back to where I came from. But first the door must be opened so I can learn the secret. I want the door to be opened! *(The POET enters.)*

LAWYER: Then you'll need to retrace your own footsteps, return the way you came, and endure all the horrors, repetitions, formalities, and reiterations of a trial.

DAUGHTER: So be it. But first I'll go into the wilderness to find myself once more. We'll meet again. *(To the POET.)* Come with me! *(Cries of lamentation are heard from the distance.)* What was that?

LAWYER: The souls of the damned on Foulstrand.

DAUGHTER: Why is their complaint more piteous today?

LAWYER: Because the sun's shining here, because there's music, because there's dancing, because there's youth! It makes their suffering all the more terrible.

DAUGHTER: Then we must free them!

LAWYER: Try if you like. A Deliverer came once—they nailed Him to a cross.

DAUGHTER: Who?

LAWYER: All right-thinking people.

DAUGHTER: Who are they?

LAWYER: You mean you don't know all the right-thinking people? Well, then, you'll have to meet some.

DAUGHTER: Are they the ones who refused you your degree?

LAWYER: Yes.

DAUGHTER: Then I know them!

(The scene changes to a Mediterranean coast. Downstage left is a white wall with orange trees in full fruit hanging over it. Upstage are villas and a casino with a terrace. To the right, a large pile of coal and two wheelbarrows. Upstage right, a strip of blue sea. Two COAL CARRIERS, bare to the waist, and with their faces, hands, and all other exposed parts blackened with coal dust, sit on the wheelbarrows in despair. The DAUGHTER and the LAWYER enter upstage.)

DAUGHTER: This is Paradise!

FIRST COAL CARRIER: This is hell!

SECOND COAL CARRIER: A hundred and twenty in the shade!

FIRST COAL CARRIER: Should we go for a swim?

SECOND COAL CARRIER: They'd only arrest us. No swimming allowed.

FIRST COAL CARRIER: Can we pick some of those oranges?

SECOND COAL CARRIER: They arrest you for that, too.

FIRST COAL CARRIER: I can't work in this heat. I'm leaving.

SECOND COAL CARRIER: Then they'd arrest you for sure! *(Pause.)* Besides, you'd have nothing to eat.

FIRST COAL CARRIER: Nothing to eat! We work the most and get the least to eat! And the rich, who do nothing, get the most! Would it be stretching the truth too far to say it's unjust? What's the Daughter of the Gods got to say to that?

DAUGHTER: I don't have an answer. But what have you done to be so black and to suffer so?

FIRST COAL CARRIER: What we've done? We were born to poor and worthless parents is what. Punished a couple times, too, I guess.

DAUGHTER: Punished?

FIRST COAL CARRIER: Yes. The unpunished sit up there in the casino eating eight course meals with wine.

DAUGHTER: *(To the LAWYER.)* Can that be true?

LAWYER: In general, yes.

DAUGHTER: You mean that at one time or other every human being does something that deserves punishment?

LAWYER: Yes.

DAUGHTER: Even you?

LAWYER: Yes.

DAUGHTER: Is it true that these poor men here can't go for a swim in the ocean?

LAWYER: That's right. Not even with their clothes on. Only those who try drowning themselves get by without paying. And more likely than not, they get beaten up at the police station.

DAUGHTER: Can't they go outside the town to swim? In the countryside?

LAWYER: There is no countryside. It's all fenced in.

DAUGHTER: I mean out in the open, where everything's free.

LAWYER: There's no such place. Everything is owned.

DAUGHTER: Even the ocean, the great wide—?

LAWYER: Everything. You can't take a boat out to sea and pull into land anywhere without being booked and fined. Wonderful, isn't it?

DAUGHTER: Then this isn't Paradise.

LAWYER: No, I assure you of that.

DAUGHTER: But why don't they improve their situation?

LAWYER: Many of them try, but all reformers end up either in jail or in the madhouse.

DAUGHTER: Who puts them in prison?

LAWYER: All right-thinking people, all respectable—

DAUGHTER: And who sends them to the madhouse?

LAWYER: Their own despair, once they see how hopeless it is.

DAUGHTER: Has no one suspected unknown reasons may be responsible?

LAWYER: Oh, yes. The well-fed have always thought so.

DAUGHTER: That it's all fine as it is—?

FIRST COAL CARRIER: And in the same breath they call us the foundation of society. If we don't deliver your coal, the fire in the kitchen goes out, the fire in the parlor goes out, machines stop in factories, street lights, lights in shops, in homes—all go out. Darkness and cold would settle on the land. And that's why we sweat like hell to deliver your black coal! And what do you give us for it?

LAWYER: *(To the DAUGHTER.)* Help them! *(Pause.)* I know things can't be equal for all, but must they be *so* unequal?

(A GENTLEMAN and LADY cross the stage.)

LADY: Wouldn't you like a round of cards?

GENTLEMAN: No, I have to walk off breakfast in preparation for lunch.

FIRST COAL CARRIER: In preparation for lunch!

SECOND COAL CARRIER: Lunch!

(CHILDREN enter and scream in terror when they see the two COAL CARRIERS.)

FIRST COAL CARRIER: They scream when they see us. They scream!

SECOND COAL CARRIER: God damn them! It's time to operate on this fucking society!

FIRST COAL CARRIER: God damn them! God damn—*(Spits in disgust.)*

LAWYER: *(To the DAUGHTER.)* It's insane! It isn't people who are so bad, it's—

DAUGHTER: What?

LAWYER: The system.

DAUGHTER: *(Hides her face and goes off.)* This isn't Paradise.

THE COAL CARRIERS. No! It's hell! Hell!

• • •

Fingal's Cave. Long green waves roll gently to the walls of the grotto. Downstage a red buoy rocks upon the waves but makes no sound except when indicated. Music of the winds. Music of the waves.

POET: Where have you brought me?

DAUGHTER: Far from the murmurs and wailings of the children of man. To the farthest ends of ocean. To this grotto we call Indra's Ear. Here, they say, the Lord of Heaven listens to the complaints of mortals.

POET: Why here?

DAUGHTER: This grotto is built like a seashell—the same as your ear—even though you've never thought about it. *(She lifts up a seashell.)* When you were a child you put a seashell to your ear and listened—listened to the rushing of your heart's blood, to the murmur of thoughts in your brain, the tearing of thousands of gentle used-up tissues in the web of your body. You hear all that in a tiny seashell. Just imagine what can be heard in this large one.

POET: *(Listens.)* All I hear is the sighing of the wind.

DAUGHTER: I'll tell you what it's saying. The lamentation of the winds.
(She speaks to soft music.)
Born in heaven's clouds,
we were chased by Indra's fires

down to this rind of Earth
that soiled our feet with its clay.
We had to endure
the dust of roads,
the cities' damps,
the stink of kitchens,
the fumes of wine.
And then, to air our lungs, we blew
out to the far stretches of the sea,
and shook our wings,
and bathed our feet.
Indra, great Lord of Heaven,
hear us!
Hear our sighs!
The Earth is not clean,
life is somber,
men are not evil,
nor are they good.
They live as they can,
from day to day.
They wander in dust,
the children of dust.
Born of dust, to dust they return.
They have no wings,
but only feet to trudge with.
They abide in dust.
Is the fault theirs?
Or is it Yours?

POET: I heard that once—

DAUGHTER: Shhh! The winds are still singing. *(She speaks to soft music.)*
We the winds, the children of air,
we bear Man's lamentations.
You have heard us on autumn evenings
in chimney stacks,
in the stovepipe,
through the crack in the window
when outside the rain
wept down the roofs;
or on winter nights,

in snow-decked woods;
or on the tossing sea.
You have heard the whine and moan
of rope and sail.
It was us You heard,
the winds, the children of air,
who in piercing the souls of men
have learned these sounds of suffering—
from the bed of the sick,
from the field of battle,
but mostly from the newborn child
who cries complaint
at the pain of life.
It is we, the winds,
that whistle and whine:
Woe, woe, woe!

POET: I think that once before—

DAUGHTER: Be still! The waves are singing. *(She speaks to soft music.)*
It is we, the waves,
that rock the winds
to rest.
Our waves, green cradles,
salty and wet,
weave like flames,
like flames of wetness;
burning, extinguishing,
bathing and cleansing,
begetting and bearing.
We, the waves,
that rock the winds
to rest.
False, faithless waves! Everything on Earth that is not burned is drowned
in those waves! Look there! *(Pointing to a heap of wreckage.)* The sea has
stolen and destroyed all this. All that remains of these ships are their fig-
ureheads—and their names: *Justice, Friendship, Golden Peace, Hope.* This
is all that is left of hope. Spars, rowlocks, bailers. And over there! The life
buoy! Saved itself, letting those in need drown!

POET: *(Rummaging in the wreckage.)* Here's the ship's nameboard. *Justice.*

The ship from Fairhaven with the Blind Man's son on board. It sank. And Alice's sweetheart was on board, too—Edith's hopeless love.

DAUGHTER: The Blind Man? Fairhaven? I must have dreamt all that. Alice's sweetheart, ugly Edith, the quarantine, sulfur and carbolic acid, the commencement, the Lawyer's office, the theater and Victoria, the Officer, the Growing Castle—I dreamt it all—

POET: I once made poetry out of such things—

DAUGHTER: Then you know what poetry is—

POET: Then I know what dreaming is. What is poetry?

DAUGHTER: Not reality, but more than reality—not a dream, but dreams dreamt in waking—

POET: And the children of man think we poets do nothing but play—invent and imagine!

DAUGHTER: And a good thing it is, too, my friend. If it were otherwise, where would encouragement be in this world? Man would lie on his back staring off into the sky. There would be no one to plow or to spade, to plane or to axe.

POET: How can you say that, Daughter of Indra, you who are of the Gods!

DAUGHTER: You're right to reproach me. I've lived down here too long, bathing in mud like you. My thoughts have forgotten how to soar; there's clay on my wings, earth on my feet, and I—*(Raising her arms.)*— I'm sinking, sinking. Help me, Father, Lord of Heaven! *(Silence.)* I don't hear Him anymore. The ether no longer carries His words to the shell of my ear. The silver thread is torn. I'm bound to earth.

POET: Will you be leaving us soon?

DAUGHTER: As soon as I've burned away this mortal matter, for the ocean's water can never wash me clean. Why do you ask?

POET: Because I have a prayer—a petition—

DAUGHTER: What petition?

POET: A petition of Man to the Ruler of the Universe, drawn up by a dreamer.

DAUGHTER: And who will deliver it?

POET: The Daughter of Indra.

DAUGHTER: Can you tell me your poem?

POET: I can.

DAUGHTER: Let me hear it.

POET: It's better if you do it.

DAUGHTER: Where will I find it?

POET: In my thoughts—or here. *(He hands her a scroll.)*

DAUGHTER: Yes. I'll say it. *(She takes the scroll, but speaks without reading.)*

"Why, O child of man,
are you born in anguish
and bring your mother pain
with the joy of motherhood,
that joy beyond all joys?
Why, when waking to life,
why must you greet the light of day
with a cry of rage and pain?
Why, O child of man,
deny life your smile,
when life should be pure joy?
Why must we who come from God
be born like animals?
Do our souls deserve no better raiment
than this of blood and filth?
Must God's image cut its teeth?"
— Shh! No! Enough!
The created must never condemn its Creator!
The riddle of life is still not solved.—
"And so the wandering begins,
over thistle, thorn and stone;
and all paths that you approach
are forever closed to you;
and every flower you bend to pick
you find to be another's.
And should a field of grain lie before you,
you will trample it under foot
to make your way less long,
knowing others will trample yours
till your loss equals theirs.
Every pleasure that life brings you
brings equal sorrow to others,
and yet your sorrow brings no pleasure.
Sorrow, sorrow piled on sorrow
will be your life till you are dead:
and your death is another's bread."
—Do you think, O son of dust,
that this will reach the Almighty's ear?
POET: How can the son of dust find words,

words pure and radiant and light,
that can tear themselves from Earth?
O Child of God, divine being,
take my poor and tattered words
and make them fit for God's own ears.

DAUGHTER: I will.

POET: *(Pointing at the buoy.)* What's that floating out there? A buoy?

DAUGHTER: Yes.

POET: It looks like a human lung with a windpipe.

DAUGHTER: It's the sea's watchman. It sings whenever there's danger.

POET: The sea appears to be rising. Waves are beginning to swell.

DAUGHTER: Not unlikely.

POET: What's that? A ship! On the rocks!

DAUGHTER: What ship can it be?

POET: The ghostship, I think.

DAUGHTER: What's that?

POET: The Flying Dutchman.

DAUGHTER: The Dutchman? Why is he so cruelly punished? And why doesn't he ever come ashore?

POET: Because he's had seven unfaithful wives.

DAUGHTER: And he has been punished for that?

POET: Yes. He's condemned by all right-thinking people.

DAUGHTER: Strange world! How can he be freed from his curse?

POET: Freed? Beware of freeing anyone!

DAUGHTER: Why?

POET: Because—No, it isn't the Dutchman. It's an ordinary ship in distress. Why doesn't the buoy sound? Look, the sea's rising, waves towering! We'll soon be imprisoned in this grotto! They're sounding the ship's bell now. Soon there'll be another ship's figurehead in here! Buoy, watchman, cry out, do your duty! *(The buoy sounds a four-part chord in fifths and sixths that resembles a foghorn.)* The crew, they're waving to us! But we'll be destroyed ourselves!

DAUGHTER: Don't you want to be freed from life?

POET: Yes, just not now! And not by water!

THE CREW: *(Singing in four parts.)* Kyrie Eleison!

POET: They're crying now! And the sea's crying, too! But no one hears!

THE CREW: *(As before.)* Kyrie Eleison!

DAUGHTER: Who is that coming out there?

POET: Walking on water? There's only One Who walks on water. It's not Peter, the rock, he sank like a stone.

(A white radiance spreads across the water.)

THE CREW. *Kyrie Eleison!*

DAUGHTER: Is it He?

POET: He. The Crucified One.

DAUGHTER: Why—tell me—why was He crucified?

POET: Because He wanted to free mankind.

DAUGHTER: I've forgotten. Who—who crucified Him?

POET: All right-thinking people.

DAUGHTER: What a strange world!

POET: The sea's rising! Darkness coming down! The storm's growing wilder!

(THE CREW cries out in fear.) They're screaming in terror at the sight of their Savior! And—and now they're jumping overboard in fear of their Redeemer! *(Another cry of fear from THE CREW.)* Now they're screaming in fear of dying. They scream at birth and they scream at death.

(The rising waves threaten to drown them in the grotto.)

DAUGHTER: If only I were sure it's a ship—

POET: You're right—I don't think it's a ship. It's a two-story house with trees in front. And—and—and a telephone tower—a tower that rises high into the clouds. The modern Tower of Babel—with wires in the clouds to communicate with the gods!

DAUGHTER: Child, men's thoughts don't need metal wires to reach heaven. A devout man's prayers penetrate all the worlds. That's no Tower of Babel. If you want to storm the heavens, storm them with your prayers.

POET: No, it's no house, no telephone tower. Do you see?

DAUGHTER: What do you see?

POET: I see a meadow covered with snow. A meadow that serves as a drill-field. The winter sun is peering out from behind the church on the hill, and its tower is casting a long shadow across the snow. And now, marching across the meadow, is a troop of soldiers. They're marching on the tower and up the spire. They're on the cross now. I have the feeling that the first to step on the weathercock must die. They're very close now. The corporal leading them on is—*(Laughs.)* A cloud has just crossed the meadow, past the sun, and—and now everything's gone! The cloud's water has put out the sun's fire! The light of the sun created the tower's shadow, but the shadow of the cloud has smothered the tower's shadow—

*(During the last speech the stage picture has changed once again to the the-
ater corridor, with the STAGE-DOOR KEEPER in her usual place. The
DAUGHTER and the POET enter.)*

DAUGHTER: *(To the STAGE-DOOR KEEPER.)* Has the Chancellor of the
University arrived yet?

STAGE-DOOR KEEPER: No.

DAUGHTER: What about the Deans?

STAGE-DOOR KEEPER: No.

DAUGHTER: Call them at once, then; the door is about to be opened!

STAGE-DOOR KEEPER: Is it that urgent?

DAUGHTER: Yes! We suspect the riddle of existence is locked up behind it.
Call the Chancellor and the Deans of the Four Faculties. *(The STAGE-
DOOR KEEPER blows a whistle.)* And don't forget the Glazier and his
diamond, or nothing will get done.

*(MEMBERS OF THE OPERA COMPANY swarm out of the theater as
earlier in the play. The OFFICER, who is young again, enters from the rear,
dressed in morning-coat and top hat, and carries a bouquet of roses. He is
radiantly happy.)*

OFFICER: *(Sings.)* Victoria!

STAGE-DOOR KEEPER: The young lady will be out soon.

OFFICER: Excellent! The carriage is waiting, the table's set, the champagne's
on ice! Madam, I should like to embrace you! *(He embraces her, then sings
out.)* Victoria!

WOMAN'S VOICE: *(Sings from above.)* I'm here!

OFFICER: *(Begins pacing about.)* All right! I'm waiting!

POET: I feel I've been through this before.

DAUGHTER: And I.

POET: Could I have dreamt it?

DAUGHTER: Or written it?

POET: Or written it?

DAUGHTER: Then you know what poetry is—

POET: Then I know what dreaming is—

DAUGHTER: I feel that once before we stood somewhere else saying these
same words.

POET: Then you'll soon know what reality is.

DAUGHTER: Or dreaming.

POET: Or poetry.

*(The CHANCELLOR and the DEANS OF THE FOUR FACULTIES:
THEOLOGY, PHILOSOPHY, MEDICINE, and LAW enter.)*

CHANCELLOR: It appears to be a question of the door. What thinks the Dean of the Theological Faculty?

DEAN OF THEOLOGY: I do not think. I believe. *Credo.*

DEAN OF PHILOSOPHY: I rationalize.

DEAN OF MEDICINE: I know.

DEAN OF LAW: I doubt—as long as we have neither evidence nor witnesses.

CHANCELLOR: So now we shall quarrel again. But to begin, what does Theology believe?

DEAN OF THEOLOGY: I believe that this door must not be opened, for it conceals dangerous truths.

DEAN OF PHILOSOPHY: Truth is never dangerous.

DEAN OF MEDICINE: What is truth?

DEAN OF LAW: Whatever can be proved by two witnesses!

DEAN OF THEOLOGY: Anything can be proved by two *false* witnesses!

DEAN OF PHILOSOPHY: Truth is wisdom. And wisdom knowledge. And Philosophy alone is both of these. Philosophy is the science of all science, the knowledge of all knowledge. And all other sciences are the servants of Philosophy.

DEAN OF MEDICINE: The sole science is natural science. Philosophy is not science, but empty speculation.

DEAN OF THEOLOGY: Bravo!

DEAN OF PHILOSOPHY: *(To the DEAN OF THEOLOGY.)* You cry bravo. But just who, if I may ask, are you? You are the archenemy of all knowledge and the adversary of all science. You are ignorance and darkness.

DEAN OF MEDICINE: Bravo!

DEAN OF THEOLOGY: *(To the DEAN OF MEDICINE.)* You, too, cry bravo, you who can see no farther than the end of your nose in a magnifying glass, who believe nothing but your deceptive senses. Your eyes, for example, that can be farsighted, nearsighted, blind, purblind, squint-eyed, color-blind, red-blind, green-blind—

DEAN OF MEDICINE: Idiot!

DEAN OF THEOLOGY: Ass!

(They attack one another.)

CHANCELLOR: Silence! One crow ought not to peck at the eyes of another crow!

DEAN OF PHILOSOPHY:. If I had to choose between the two of them, Theology and Medicine, I would choose—neither.

DEAN OF LAW: And if I had to sit in judgment over you three, I would convict—every one of you! You are unable to agree on any single point, and you have *never* been able to. But now let us return to the problem. What is the Chancellor's opinion of this door and of the opening of it?

CHANCELLOR: Opinion? I have no opinion. I have been appointed by the government merely to see that you here on the council do not break one another's arms and legs while you are educating the young. Opinions? Oh, I guard against having opinions. I had a number of them once, but they were immediately refuted. Opinions are always immediately refuted—by one's opponents, of course.—What do you think? Are we to allow the opening of the door? Even at the risk of dangerous truths behind it?

DEAN OF LAW: What is truth? Where is truth?

DEAN OF THEOLOGY: I am the Truth and the Life—

DEAN OF PHILOSOPHY: I am the Knowledge of Knowledge—

DEAN OF MEDICINE: I am Exact Knowledge—

DEAN OF LAW: I doubt!

(They attack one another.)

DAUGHTER: Shame on you, teachers of the young!

DEAN OF LAW: Lord Chancellor, as advisor to the government, and head of the faculty, I ask you to denounce this woman for her offense! She has cried shame upon you, and that is an affront! And she has ironically referred to you as "teachers of the young," which is no less than libelous!

DAUGHTER: I pity the young!

DEAN OF LAW: She pities the young, which is as much as to say she accuses *us!* Lord Chancellor, you will denounce that woman!

DAUGHTER: Yes, I accuse you, all of you, of sowing doubt and dissension in the minds of the young!

DEAN OF LAW: Listen to her! She herself wakes doubts in the minds of the young in regard to our authority! And yet she has the gall to accuse *us* of waking doubts! I ask you in the name of all right-thinking people, is this not a criminal offense?

ALL RIGHTEOUS MEN: Yes, it is criminal!

DEAN OF LAW: All right-thinking people have condemned you. Go in peace with what you have won, or—

DAUGHTER: What have I won? Or— ? Or what?

DEAN OF LAW: Or else you will be struck.

POET: Or crucified.

DAUGHTER: *(To the POET.)* I'm going. Follow me and you'll learn the riddle's answer.

POET: Riddle?

DAUGHTER: What did he mean by what I have "won"?

POET: Probably nothing. We call that idle talk. He was just talking.

DAUGHTER: But he hurt me deeply by saying it.

POET: Why else would he have said it? People do things like that.

ALL RIGHT-THINKING PEOPLE: Hurrah! The door is opened!

CHANCELLOR: And what is concealed behind it?

GLAZIER: Nothing that I can see.

CHANCELLOR: He doesn't see a thing! Well, I can certainly believe that. My Deans will tell me what is behind the door.

DEAN OF THEOLOGY: Nothing. That is the answer to the riddle of existence. In the beginning God created heaven and earth out of Nothing.

DEAN OF PHILOSOPHY: Nothing will come of nothing.

DEAN OF MEDICINE: Nonsense! There's nothing here.

DEAN OF LAW: I doubt that. And I smell a fraud. I appeal to all right-thinking people!

DAUGHTER: *(To the POET.)* Who are these right-thinking people?

POET: Good question! Often all right-thinking people boil down to just one. Today it's me and mine, tomorrow it's you and yours. One is nominated to the honor, or, more correctly, nominates oneself.

ALL RIGHT-THINKING PEOPLE: We have been deceived!

CHANCELLOR: And who has deceived you?

ALL RIGHT-THINKING PEOPLE: The Daughter!

CHANCELLOR: *(To the DAUGHTER.)* Will you kindly tell us why you had the door opened?

DAUGHTER: No, my friends. If I told you, you would never believe me.

DEAN OF MEDICINE: But there's nothing there.

DAUGHTER: You're quite right. But do you understand this Nothing?

DEAN OF MEDICINE: She's talking nonsense!

ALL: Nonsense!

DAUGHTER: *(To the POET.)* They're to be pitied.

POET: You're serious?

DAUGHTER: I'm always serious.

POET: Then you pity the right-thinking, too?

DAUGHTER: Perhaps them must of all.

POET: And the Four Faculties?

DAUGHTER: Yes, and by no means least. Four heads with four minds on one body! Who created this monster?

ALL: She does not answer?

CHANCELLOR: Then strike her!

DAUGHTER: I *have* answered!

CHANCELLOR: Listen to her! She's answering!

ALL: Strike her! She's answering!

DAUGHTER: Yes! Strike her whether she answers or not! *(To the POET.)* Come, seer. I'll answer this riddle for you, just not here, but far away in the wilderness, with no one to hear, no one to see, because—

(The LAWYER goes to the DAUGHTER and grabs her by the arm.)

LAWYER: Haven't you forgotten your duties?

DAUGHTER: No, I haven't, but I have higher ones!

LAWYER: And your child?

DAUGHTER: My child? What else?

LAWYER: Your child is calling for you.

DAUGHTER: My child! O God, I'm earthbound! And this torment inside me, this fear! What is it?

LAWYER: Don't you know?

DAUGHTER: No!

LAWYER: The pangs of conscience!

DAUGHTER: The pangs of conscience?

LAWYER: Yes! They come haunting after every neglected duty, after every pleasure, however innocent—if there is such a thing as innocent pleasure, which is doubtful—and after every pain caused to another.

DAUGHTER: And is there no cure?

LAWYER: Yes, only one—to fulfill the duty at once.

DAUGHTER: When you say that word "duty" you look like a demon. But what if I have two duties?

LAWYER: You first fulfill the one, then the other.

DAUGHTER: But the highest first. And so I leave my child in your care while I fulfill my duty.

LAWYER: Your child is unhappy, he misses you. Can't you see? Another human is suffering on your account—

DAUGHTER: You've sown dissension in my soul! I'm torn in two!

LAWYER: These are what we call life's petty trials.

DAUGHTER: They're tearing me inside!

POET: If you had any idea of the grief and destruction I've spread in following my own calling—yes, calling, the highest of duties—you'd never take my hand.

DAUGHTER: I don't know what you're saying.

POET: I had a father who placed all his hopes in me, his only son, who was to carry on his business. But I ran away from business school and my father died of grief. My mother wanted me to become a minister, but I couldn't, and she disowned me. I had a friend who helped me through my most difficult times. But that friend acted like a tyrant toward those very people I spoke and sang for. To save my soul I had to destroy my friend and benefactor. Since that day I've had no peace of mind; people think me contemptible and the scum of the earth; and it doesn't help when my conscience says "You did right!" for the very next moment it says "You did wrong!" Such is life.

DAUGHTER: Follow me into the wilderness.

LAWYER: Your child!

DAUGHTER: *(Pointing to all those present.)* These are my children! In themselves each one is good, but bring them together and they turn into demons. Good-bye!

(After a blackout, the lights come up again on the scene outside the Castle as at the beginning, except that now the ground around the wall is covered with blue monkshoods. The bud of the chrysanthemum at the top of the Castle is on the verge of bursting into blossom. The Castle windows are lighted with candles. A fire burns downstage. The DAUGHTER and the POET are onstage.)

DAUGHTER: The time is near when with the help of fire I will ascend again into the ether. It's what you mortals call death, and which you approach with such fear.

POET: Fear of the unknown.

DAUGHTER: Which you know.

POET: Who knows it?

DAUGHTER: Every one of you. Why can't you believe your prophets?

POET: No one has ever believed prophets. Why is that? Why? "If God has spoken, why don't people believe?" His power to convince must be irresistible.

DAUGHTER: Have you always been a doubter?

POET: No. I've had times of certainty, but not for long. They soon passed, like a dream upon waking.

DAUGHTER: It isn't easy being human!

POET: Do you understand that now?

DAUGHTER: Yes!

POET: Tell me, wasn't it Indra who once sent down his Son to hear the complaints of man?

DAUGHTER: Yes. And how was He received?

POET: How did He fulfill His mission, if I may answer with a question?

DAUGHTER: And I'll reply with another question. Wasn't the estate of man bettered because of His visit?

POET: Bettered? Yes, a bit. A very little bit. But instead of all these questions, won't you answer the riddle?

DAUGHTER: Yes. But why? You won't believe me.

POET: I *will* believe you, because I know who you are!

DAUGHTER: All right. I'll tell you. At the dawn of time, before even the sun shone, Brahma, the divine primal force, invited His own seduction by Maya, the world mother, to multiply Himself. This union of the divine substance with the substance of earth was the fall from grace. The world, life, and mankind are no more than a mirage, an empty illusion, a dream—

POET: My dream.

DAUGHTER: A true dream! But to free themselves from this earthly substance, the children of Brahma seek self-denial and suffering. And so, suffering becomes the Deliverer. But this instinct for suffering conflicts with the pleasure principle, with joy, with love. And now you understand what love is. The supremest joy in the greatest suffering. The sweetest contained in the most bitter. Do you understand what woman is? Woman, through whom sin and death entered into life?

POET: I understand. And the end?

DAUGHTER: You already know that. The struggle between the pain of joy and the joy of pain. Between the torment of the penitent and the pleasure of the sensualist.

POET: And the struggle?

DAUGHTER: The struggle of opposites produces power, just as fire and water generate steam.

POET: But peace? Rest?

DAUGHTER: Shh! No more questions, no more answers! The altar is laid out for the sacrifice—flowers stand guard—candles lit—white sheets at the windows—and fir twigs at the entrance.

POET: You say that as peacefully as if suffering didn't exist for you.

DAUGHTER: Not exist? I suffered your sufferings a hundredfold, for my senses are infinitely sharper.

POET: Tell me your sorrows!

DAUGHTER: Poet, if you told me yours and there was a word for every grief, how close would your words be to the truth?

POET: You're right. No. I never seemed more than a deaf-mute to myself.

And when crowds of people listened in wonder to the songs I sang them, my words sounded like so much empty babble. I always blushed with shame when people praised me.

DAUGHTER: And yet you want *me* to—Look into my eyes.

POET: I couldn't bear your gaze—

DAUGHTER: Then how could you bear to hear if I spoke in my language?

POET: At least tell me one thing before you go. What caused you the greatest suffering?

DAUGHTER: Being—being human. To feel my sight grow weak by having eyes, my hearing dulled by having ears, and my thoughts, my buoyant, luminous thoughts, held prisoner by labyrinthine layers of fat. Surely you've seen a brain with all its twisting ways and secret turnings.

POET: And that's why all right-thinking people's minds are twisted.

DAUGHTER: You're cruel, always cruel, every one of you.

POET: Do we have a choice?

DAUGHTER: First I shake the dust from my feet—the earth—the clay— *(Removes her shoes and places them in the fire.)*

STAGE-DOOR KEEPER: *(Enters and puts her shawl in the fire.)* Would you mind if I added my shawl to the fire? *(Goes.)*

OFFICER: *(Enters.)* And my roses—now nothing but thorns? *(Goes.)*

BILL-POSTER: *(Enters.)* My posters, yes—my fishnet, never! *(Goes.)*

GLAZIER: *(Enters.)* Diamond that opened the door, farewell! *(Goes.)*

LAWYER: *(Enters.)* The great lawsuit in the matter of the Pope's beard and the diminishing water supply at the sources of the Ganges! *(Goes.)*

QUARANTINE MASTER: *(Enters.)* A small token—the black mask that made me a blackamoor against my will! *(Goes.)*

VICTORIA: *(Enters.)* My beauty, my sorrow! *(Goes.)*

EDITH: My ugliness, my sorrow! *(Goes.)*

BLIND MAN: *(Enters and holds his hand in the fire.)* My hand—my sight! *(Goes.)*
(The DANDY is pushed in seated in his wheelchair. The COQUETTE and the FRIEND are with him.)

DANDY: Hurry, hurry, life is short! *(The three go out.)*
(The DAUGHTER and the POET remain alone.)

POET: I've read that when life nears its end everyone and everything rushes past in a rapid stream.—Is this the end?

DAUGHTER: It is for me. Good-bye!

POET: No parting word?

DAUGHTER: I can't. No. How could your words ever express our thoughts?

DEAN OF THEOLOGY: *(Storms in, raging.)* God has deceived me, man persecutes me, the government has abandoned me, and my colleagues scorn me! How am I to have faith when no one else has faith? How am I to defend a God who does not defend His own? It's all nonsense! *(Throws a book onto the fire and goes.)*

POET: *(Tearing the book from the fire.)* Do you know what the book was? A book of martyrs. A calendar with a martyr designated for each day of the year.

DAUGHTER: A martyr?

POET: Yes, someone who was tortured and killed for his faith! But can you tell me why? Do you believe that all who are tortured suffer, and that all who are killed feel pain? Suffering *must* be redemption and death deliverance!

KRISTIN: *(Enters with strips of paper in her hands.)* I'm pasting, I'm pasting, till there's nothing more to paste—

POET: If heaven cracked open you'd try pasting *it* shut, too! Get out of here!

KRISTIN. Aren't there any double windows in the Castle?

POET: No!

KRISTIN: *(Going.)* I'll go, then! I'll go!

DAUGHTER: It's time. The end has come.
    Farewell, child of man, dreamer,
    Poet, you know what way of life
    is best. Soaring on wings you hover
    above the Earth, and then dip down
    to touch the dust, but only to touch it,
    and then soar high again. But now
    the hour of parting has come,
    the time to leave behind both friends
    and earthly things that I have loved.
    How can I not feel the loss
    of parting, and a deeper regret
    of all that is destroyed. I know
    the suffering of being now,
    the heavy yoke of humankind:
    to feel the loss of the never-prized,
    to feel remorse for the never-done,
    to long to go and yet to stay.
    And so the heart is split in two—
    torn by two wild horses,

by conflict, discord, and uncertainty.
Good-bye. And tell your mortal brothers
that I will not forget them,
but remember them where I am going,
and will carry your lamentations,
in your name, to the throne of God.
Farewell!

(She goes into the Castle. Music is heard. The background is illuminated by the burning of the Castle, till finally we see a wall of questioning, mourning, grieving faces. While the Castle burns, the bud on the roof bursts open and becomes a gigantic chrysanthemum.)

END OF PLAY

THE GHOST
SONATA

1907

Cast of Characters

THE OLD MAN *Hummel*

THE STUDENT *Arkenholz*

THE MILKMAID *an apparition*

THE DARK LADY *daughter of the Dead Man and the Caretaker's Wife*

THE CARETAKER'S WIFE

THE COLONEL

THE MUMMY *the Colonel's wife, the Daughter's mother*

THE FIANCÉE *formerly engaged to the Old Man*

THE DAUGHTER *supposedly the Colonel's daughter, but in reality the
Old Man's*

THE DEAD MAN *a consul*

THE ARISTOCRAT *engaged to the Dark Lady*

JOHANSSON *the servant of the Old Man*

BENGTSSON *the Colonel's servant*

MISS BEATA VON HOLSTEINKRONA *The Old Man's former fiancée*

THE HOUSEMAID

THE COOK

BEGGARS

The Ghost Sonata

SCENE ONE

The corner façade of a modern apartment building showing the ground and first story. At the corner of the ground floor is a round living room. Above it, on the first story, a balcony with a flagpole. When the blinds at the open window of the Round Room are raised, the white marble statue of a young woman is seen surrounded by palms and brightly lighted by the rays of the sun. The window to the left is lined with pink, blue, and white hyacinths. Across the railing of the balcony hang a comforter of blue silk and two white pillows. The windows to the left are covered with white sheets. It is a bright Sunday morning. Downstage in front of the house is a green bench. Downstage right, a small fountain; left, an advertising kiosk. Upstage left is the main house door, and through it the staircase is seen with its banisters of mahogany and brass. On the sidewalk to either side of the house door are containers with laurel trees planted in them. The corner in which the Round Room is situated looks out onto a side street that leads upstage. To the left of the house door is a window with a window mirror, with the aid of which events at the front of the house may be observed. At the rise of the curtain the sounds of numerous church bells are heard in the distance.

The house door is open. The DARK LADY stands motionless on the staircase. The CARETAKER'S WIFE is sweeping the doorstep. She then polishes the brass doorknob, and finally waters the laurels. At the kiosk the OLD MAN sits in a wheelchair and reads a newspaper. His hair and beard are white and he wears glasses. The MILKMAID comes around the corner carrying milk bottles in a wire basket. She wears a summer dress, brown shoes, black stockings, and a white cap which she removes and hangs on the fountain. She wipes the perspiration from her forehead and drinks from the cup fastened to the fountain by a chain. Finally she washes her hands and arranges her hair using the surface of the water as a mirror. A steamship bell sounds, and from time to time the deep tones of an organ in a neighboring church break the silence. After several moments of this silence, when the MILKMAID has finished her toilet, the STUDENT, who has not slept and is unshaven, enters from the left. He goes directly to the fountain and, after a pause, speaks.

STUDENT: May I use the cup? *(The MILKMAID pulls the cup to herself as if guarding it.)* Haven't you almost finished? *(She looks at him frightened.)*

OLD MAN: *(To himself.)* Who is he talking to? I don't see anyone. Is he mad? *(He continues to watch the STUDENT with great astonishment.)*

STUDENT: *(To the MILKMAID.)* Why are you looking at me like that? Do I look all that bad? Fact is, I haven't been to bed, and you probably think I've been out on a binge. *(She stares at him with the same expression.)* That's what you think, isn't it? Do I have whiskey on my breath? *(Her expression doesn't change.)* I haven't shaved, I know—Hey, how about a drink of water? Don't worry, I've earned it. *(Pause.)* I suppose I ought to tell you I spent all night dressing wounds and taking care of the injured. So now you know. *(She rinses out the cup, fills it, and hands it to him.)* Thank you. *(She remains motionless.)* Would you do me a great favor? *(Pause.)* The fact is, my eyes are all swollen, as you can see, and since I've been handling wounds and dead bodies, I really shouldn't get my hands close to my eyes. Would you dip my clean handkerchief in fresh water and bathe them for me? Would you do that? Would you play the Good Samaritan? *(She hesitates for a moment, then does what he has asked.)* Thank you, my friend. *(He takes out a purse but she makes a gesture of refusal.)* I'm sorry, how thoughtless! I'm asleep on my feet. *(The MILK-MAID disappears.)*

OLD MAN: *(To the STUDENT.)* You'll excuse me, I couldn't help overhearing. You say you were at the scene of the accident last night? I've just been reading about it.

STUDENT: So soon?

OLD MAN: Yes. The whole story. Even a picture of you. They regret not knowing the name of the brave student who—

STUDENT: *(Looking at the paper.)* That's me, all right!

OLD MAN: Who were you talking to just now?

STUDENT: Didn't you see her? *(Pause.)*

OLD MAN: Would it be rude if I asked—well, had the honor of knowing— your name?

STUDENT: What good would that do? I try to avoid publicity, you see. The moment you turn famous, they start saying terrible things about you. Character assassination has become an art these days. Besides, I'm not looking for a reward.

OLD MAN: You're well off, then—

STUDENT: Afraid not. Actually I'm poor as a pauper.

OLD MAN: Wait! Yes! I think I know that voice. I had a friend once, long ago, who pronounced it just that way. He said "pore" instead of "poor." Pore as a pauper. Are you by any chance related to a merchant by the name of Arkenholz?

STUDENT: He was my father.

OLD MAN: Strange are the paths of fate! I saw you once when you were only a child. Unfortunately, the circumstances weren't exactly happy.

STUDENT: Yes, they tell me I was born into a bankrupt family.

OLD MAN: Indeed you were.

STUDENT: May I ask your name?

OLD MAN: My name is Hummel.

STUDENT: You—? Yes—yes, I remember—

OLD MAN: You've often heard my name, I'm sure.

STUDENT: Yes—

OLD MAN: With a certain—aversion, perhaps? *(The STUDENT is silent.)* Yes, I can believe that. I'm supposed to have been the one who ruined your father. Everyone who is ruined by stupid speculations always claims he was ruined by the very person he was unable to fool. *(Pause.)* The fact of the matter is that your father cheated me out of seventeen thousand crowns. At the time, that was everything I had.

STUDENT: How can two versions of a single story differ so?

OLD MAN: Do you think I'm lying?

STUDENT: How can I not? My father never lied.

OLD MAN: That's true. Fathers never lie. But I'm a father myself—and so—

STUDENT: What are you trying to say, exactly?

OLD MAN: I saved your father from disaster, and my reward was his terrible hatred, rather than the gratitude he owed me. He taught his family to despise the ground I walked on.

STUDENT: Perhaps you poisoned your help with unnecessary humiliations?

OLD MAN: All help is humiliating, sir.

STUDENT: What do you want from me?

OLD MAN: I'm not asking for money. But if you'll do me a small service, I'll consider the debt paid in full. As you see, I'm a cripple. Some say it's my own fault. Others blame my parents. But I'd rather think that life itself, with its small, malicious pranks, is to blame. You escape one trap and immediately fall into another. In any case, I don't run up and down stairs, and I don't ring doorbells. And so I ask you, will you help me?

STUDENT: What can I do?

OLD MAN: To begin with, push my chair so I can read the playbills. I want to see what's playing at the theater.

STUDENT: *(Pushing his wheelchair.)* Don't you have an attendant?

OLD MAN: He's busy just now—on an errand. Be right back, though.—Are you a medical student?

STUDENT: I study languages. But I've no idea what I want to become.

OLD MAN: Aha! What do you know about mathematics?

STUDENT: Quite a lot, actually.

OLD MAN: Good. What would you say to a job?

STUDENT: Why not? Sure!

OLD MAN: Excellent! *(Reading the playbills.)* They're playing *Die Walküre* this afternoon. That means the Colonel will be there with his daughter. And since they always sit at the end of the sixth row, I'll get you a seat next to them. You will now be so kind as to go to that telephone booth and order seat number eighty-two in the sixth row.

STUDENT: I'm going to the opera this afternoon?

OLD MAN: Yes. Do as I tell you and you'll come off rather well. I want to see you happy, rich, and respected. Your debut last night in the role of hero will make you famous by tomorrow, and your name will be worth a fortune.

STUDENT: *(Going to the telephone booth.)* I must say, this isn't business as usual.

OLD MAN: Are you a gambler?

STUDENT: Unfortunately.

OLD MAN: This time it will be fortunately. Go make the call.

(The STUDENT goes to the telephone booth. The OLD MAN reads the newspaper. The DARK LADY has come out onto the sidewalk and speaks with the CARETAKER'S WIFE. The OLD MAN listens, but the audience hears nothing. The STUDENT returns.)

STUDENT: Done.

OLD MAN: Do you see that house there?

STUDENT: Yes, I've noticed it. When I came by yesterday, the sun was shining on the windowpanes. I imagined to myself all the beautiful, elegant things there must be inside, and I said to my friend: "Just think of living up there on the fifth floor, with a young, beautiful wife and two lovely children, and an income of twenty thousand crowns a year!"

OLD MAN: Is that really what you said? You really said that? Yes, well—I love that house, too.

STUDENT: Do you speculate in houses?

OLD MAN: Mm. Yes. But not in the way you might think.

STUDENT: You know the people who live there?

OLD MAN: Every one of them. At my age you get to know everyone. Not withstanding fathers and grandfathers. And, strangely enough, you find you're somehow related to them. I'm eighty years old, but no one really knows me well. I take an interest in the destiny of man— *(The blinds in the Round Room are raised. The COLONEL appears wearing civilian clothes. After looking at the thermometer, he goes back into the room, but stops in front of the marble statue.)* Look! That's the Colonel! The one you'll be sitting next to this afternoon.

STUDENT: Him? The Colonel? I really don't understand all this. It's like a fairy tale.

OLD MAN: My life, my dear boy, has been a book of fairy tales. The stories may be different, but a single thread runs through them all, a leitmotiv that constantly recurs.

STUDENT: That marble statue in there—who's it of?

OLD MAN: His wife, naturally.

STUDENT: Was she really that beautiful?

OLD MAN: Mm—yes. Yes.

STUDENT: Tell me about it.

OLD MAN: My dear boy, there's no way to judge our fellow mortals. Impossible. And if I told you he beat her, that she left him and then returned, that he married her a second time, and now she sits there like a mummy, worshipping her own statue—you'd think me crazy.

STUDENT: I don't understand.

OLD MAN: I can believe that! Well, now! Over there we have the hyacinth window. That's where his daughter lives. She's out for a ride just now, but she'll soon be back.

STUDENT: And the lady talking to the caretaker's wife?

OLD MAN: Ah, well, that's a bit complicated. But it's all tied in with the dead man upstairs there—where you see the white sheets.

STUDENT: Who was he?

OLD MAN: A human being, no different from the rest of us. His most notable attribute was his vanity. If you were a Sunday's child, you would see him come out that door only to look at the consulate flag flying at half-mast. He was a consul, you see—liked nothing better than crowns, lions, plumed hats and colored ribbons.

STUDENT: Sunday's child? I was born on a Sunday.

OLD MAN: No! Were you really? I should have known that. I can tell by the color of your eyes. But that means you can see what—what others cannot see. Have you noticed that?

STUDENT: Well, I don't know what other's see, exactly, but at times—I'd just as soon not talk about it.

OLD MAN: Ah, I was certain of it! I just knew! But you can talk about it to me. After all, I understand these things.

STUDENT: Yesterday, for example—I was drawn to that out-of-the-way little street where the house collapsed. I walked down it and stopped in front of a building I'd never seen before. I then noticed a crack in the wall, and then the floor beams started to snap. I ran over and grabbed up a child who was just about to pass the wall, and then it collapsed— the house. I was safe, but—but when I looked into my arms where I thought I held the child—there was nothing—

OLD MAN: Ah! Remarkable! Remarkable! I believe you! I guessed as much! But you must explain something to me. Why were you making such gestures just now at the fountain?

STUDENT: You didn't see me talking to the milkmaid?

OLD MAN: *(Horrified.)* Milkmaid?!

STUDENT: Yes, she handed me the cup.

OLD MAN: Of course. So that was it. Well, such things I cannot see. But there are other things that I can do— *(A white-haired old woman, the FIANCÉE, appears and sits at the window, beside the window mirror.)* Do you see the old woman there at the window? Do you see her? She was my fiancée sixty years ago. I was twenty. You needn't be afraid, she doesn't recognize me. We see each other every day, but it means nothing to me, even though we once vowed to love each other eternally. Eternally!

STUDENT: How foolish people in your time must have been! Nowadays we'd never make such a promise to a girl!

OLD MAN: Forgive us, young man. We didn't know any better. But can't you see how young and beautiful the old woman must have been?

STUDENT: Not really. Well, maybe—there's a certain something there—an expression. But I can't see her eyes.

(The CARETAKER'S WIFE comes out with the basket and strews the sidewalk with fir twigs, customary for a funeral.)

OLD MAN: Aha, the caretaker's wife! The dark lady is her daughter, by the dead man upstairs. That's how her husband got to be caretaker. But the dark lady has a suitor, an aristocrat, and hopes to make a wealthy marriage. Meanwhile, he's in the process of getting a divorce from his present wife, and she's giving him a fine house just to get rid of him. This aristocratic suitor is the son-in-law of the dead man, and you can see his bedclothes being aired up there on the balcony. I must say, it's all a rather complicated business.

STUDENT: I should say.

OLD MAN: Yes, inside and out, both, simple as it may appear.

STUDENT: But, then, who is the dead man?

OLD MAN: You asked me that once and I answered you. If you could see around the corner right now to the back entrance, you'd find a crowd of beggars that he used to help—whenever it took his fancy.

STUDENT: He was a kind man, then?

OLD MAN: At times.

STUDENT: Not always?

OLD MAN: That's life. But now, my boy, would you push my chair so I can catch the sun. When you don't move about, the blood congeals. Besides, I'm going to die soon. I know that. But before I do, I still have some things that need doing. Give me your hand. Feel how cold I am.

STUDENT: *(Takes his hand.)* How terrible!

OLD MAN: Don't leave me. I'm weak and lonely. But, you see, I wasn't always this way. I have an infinitely long life behind me—an infinitely long life. I've made people unhappy, and people have made me unhappy. The one cancels out the other. But before I die, I want to make you happy. Our destinies are more than casually involved—through your father—and other things.

STUDENT: Let go of my hand! You're draining my strength! I'm freezing! What do you want?

OLD MAN: Your patience. You'll understand soon enough. Here comes the young lady!

STUDENT: The Colonel's daughter?

OLD MAN: Yes! Look at her! Have you ever beheld such a masterpiece?

STUDENT: She looks like the marble statue inside.

OLD MAN: It's her mother!

STUDENT: Of course! You're right! I've never seen such a woman! What a wife and home she'd make for some man!

OLD MAN: You can see that, yes. But not everyone recognizes her beauty. Good, then, that's how it's to be. *(The DAUGHTER enters in an English riding habit. Seeing no one, she goes slowly to the door, stops, says a few words to the CARETAKER'S WIFE, then disappears into the house. The STUDENT places his hand over his eyes.)* Are you crying?

STUDENT: What can I do but despair? It's all so hopeless.

OLD MAN: I can open doors and human hearts—if only I find an arm to do my will. Serve me, and you'll have the power—

STUDENT: What is this, a devil's bargain? Am I to sell my soul?

OLD MAN: Sell nothing. Look! All my life I've done nothing but take! Now I want to give! Give! But no one will accept what I offer. I'm rich—very rich—but I have no heirs. Except, of course, for a good-for-nothing son who torments me to death. Be my son. Be my heir while I'm still alive. Enjoy life and I'll watch you enjoy it—though only from a distance.

STUDENT: What am I to do?

OLD MAN: First go to see *Die Walküre* this afternoon.

STUDENT: That's taken care of. What next?

OLD MAN: This evening you're to be in there—in the Round Room.

STUDENT: But how do I get in?

OLD MAN: By way of *Die Walküre.*

STUDENT: Why did you choose me as your medium? Did you know me before?

OLD MAN: Of course. Yes. I've had my eye on you for some time. Ah, but look up there. The maid's hoisting the flag to half-mast on the balcony, and now she's turning the bedclothes. Do you see the blue silk comforter? It was made for two to sleep under, but only one sleeps under it now— *(The DAUGHTER, who in the meanwhile has changed into a dress, appears at the window and waters the hyacinths.)* There's my little love. Just look at her. She's talking to the flowers. Isn't she like a blue hyacinth herself? She gives the flowers a drink, only the purest water, and they transform it into color and fragrance. Here comes the Colonel with his paper. He's reading her the report of the house that collapsed. He's pointing at your picture! She's moved by it. She's reading of your heroic deed! Ah, but it's clouding over. What if it starts to rain? Fine kettle of fish I'll be in if Johansson doesn't come back soon. *(It grows dark. The FIANCÉE at the window mirror closes the window.)* My fiancée's closing her window. Seventy-nine years. The window mirror is the only one she ever uses. She doesn't see herself in it, that's why—only the outside world, from both directions. Except that the world can see her. She hasn't thought of that. Anyway, she's a lovely old woman.

(The DEAD MAN appears in the doorway in his winding-sheet.)

STUDENT: Good God, what's that?

OLD MAN: What do you see?

STUDENT: Don't *you* see him? There, in the doorway, the dead man!

OLD MAN: I see nothing. But I've expected this. Tell me what you see.

STUDENT: He's coming out—onto the street— *(Pause.)* Now he's turning around and looking up at the flag.

OLD MAN: What did I tell you? And now he'll count the funeral wreaths and read the visiting cards. I pity the man whose card is missing!

STUDENT: Now he's going around the house.

OLD MAN: Off to count the beggars at the back door! The poor are a kind of decoration. "Followed to his grave by the blessings of many!" the papers will say. Well, he'll never have my blessing. Just between you and me, he was a great scoundrel.

STUDENT: But charitable.

OLD MAN: A charitable scoundrel who always dreamed of a magnificent funeral. When he felt his end approaching, he cheated the state out of another fifty thousand. Now his daughter is about to marry another woman's husband, and wonders whether she's inherited anything. That scoundrel hears everything we say. It serves him right!—Here comes Johansson. *(JOHANSSON enters from the left.)* Well? Report! *(JOHANSSON speaks to him without the audience hearing.)* Not at home? What an ass you are!—And the telegraph office?—Nothing.—Go on!—At six this evening. That's good.—Special edition?—His name in full, you say! Arkenholz, a student, born—parents—Excellent!—I think it's beginning to rain.—What did he say?—I see. He doesn't want to. —Then he must.—Here comes the aristocratic gentlemen.—Wheel me around the corner so that I can hear what the beggars are saying. And as for you, Arkenholz, wait here for me.—Hurry, Johansson, hurry! *(JOHANSSON pushes the chair around the corner. The STUDENT remains behind and watches the DAUGHTER, who is now loosening the earth in the flower pots. The ARISTOCRAT enters in mourning and speaks to the DARK LADY walking up and down on the pavement.)*

ARISTOCRAT: What can we do about it? We shall have to wait.

LADY: I can't wait!

ARISTOCRAT: I see. Then go to the country.

LADY: I don't want to!

ARISTOCRAT: Come over here! They'll hear what we're saying! *(He pulls her toward the kiosk where they continue their conversation inaudibly.)*

JOHANSSON: *(Enters from the right; to the STUDENT.)* My master asks you not to forget the other matter, sir.

STUDENT: *(Hesitantly.)* Listen—tell me—who *is* your master?

JOHANSSON: Well, you see, he's a *lot* of things, and he's *been everything*.

STUDENT: Is he sane?

JOHANSSON: That depends. He's spent his entire life looking for a Sunday's child—or so he says. That needn't be true, of course.

STUDENT: Then what does he want? Is he a miser?

JOHANSSON: He wants power. All day long he rides around in his chariot like the god Thor himself. He looks at houses, has them torn down, builds up squares, opens new streets. He also breaks into houses, sneaks through windows, plays havoc with men's destinies, kills his enemies, and forgives no one. Could you imagine this cripple was once a Don Juan, even though he always lost his women?

STUDENT: How do you explain that?

JOHANSSON: He's so sly, you see, he manages it so that women leave him just when he becomes bored with them. At the moment he's more like a horse thief except that he deals in humans. He steals people in various ways. Myself, for example, he literally stole from the hands of the law. The thing is, I made a small slipup. Something only he knew about. Instead of throwing me in jail, he made me his slave. I slave for him only for my food, and that's nothing to brag about.

STUDENT: What will he do with this house?

JOHANSSON: I'd rather not say. It's all terribly complicated.

STUDENT: I think I'd better get out of this while I still can.

JOHANSSON: Look at that! The young lady's dropped her bracelet from the window. (*The STUDENT walks over slowly, picks up the bracelet, and hands it to the DAUGHTER, who thanks him stiffly. The STUDENT returns to JOHANSSON.*) So you're thinking of skipping out. It's not as easy as you might think, once he's got you in his net. Nothing between heaven and earth frightens him. Except for one thing. Or rather, one person—

STUDENT: Wait—I think I know.

JOHANSSON: How could you know that?

STUDENT: I'm guessing. Is it—is it a little milkmaid that he's afraid of?

JOHANSSON: Well, he does turn his head away whenever he sees a milk cart. Besides, he talks in his sleep. It seems he was once in Hamburg—

STUDENT: Can this man be trusted?

JOHANSSON: You can believe everything he says.

STUDENT: What's he doing around the corner there?

JOHANSSON: Listening to the beggars. He sows a word, and picks at each stone in the house one by one, until the house collapses. Figuratively speaking, of course. I'm an educated man, you see. I was once a book-seller. Do you still want out?

STUDENT: I don't like being ungrateful. This man once saved my father. And all he asks of me now is a small service in return.

JOHANSSON: Service?

STUDENT: I'm to go to the theater today. To hear *Die Walküre.*

JOHANSSON: I don't understand. But he always comes up with new devices. Look there. Now he's calling to the policeman. He's always in good with the police. Makes demands upon them, involves them in his interests, deceives them with false promises and false pretenses. And all this just to sound them out. You'll see—before this day is out he'll be received in the Round Room.

STUDENT: What does he want in there? What's between him and the Colonel?

JOHANSSON: Yes, well, I have my suspicions, but I know nothing definite. You'll see for yourself once you're inside.

STUDENT: I'll never get in there.

JOHANSSON: That depends on you. Go to *Die Walküre,*

STUDENT: That's the way, then?

JOHANSSON: Yes, if that's what he said. Look at him over there, in his war chariot, drawn in triumph by the beggars! And they'll get nothing for their efforts. Except maybe a hint of something at his funeral.

OLD MAN: *(Enters standing in his wheelchair, drawn by a BEGGAR, with all the others following.)* Hail to this noble youth, who with danger to his life saved so many in yesterday's accident! Hail, Arkenholz! *(The BEGGARS remove their caps, but say nothing. The DAUGHTER in the window waves her handkerchief. The COLONEL gazes from his window. The FIANCÉE rises at her window. The MAID on the balcony hoists the flag to the top of the mast.)* Clap your hands, citizens! To be sure, it is Sunday, but the ass at the draw-well and the ear of corn in the field will absolve us. And although I am not a Sunday's child, I do possess the gift of prophesy and healing, for once I brought a drowned man back to life. That was in Hamburg. On a Sunday morning. Just like this one— *(The MILKMAID appears, seen only by the STUDENT and the OLD MAN. She stretches her arms above her like a person drowning, and gazes fixedly at the OLD MAN, who sinks horror-struck into his chair.)* Johansson! Take me away! Quick! Arkenholz, don't forget. *Die Walküre.*

STUDENT: What is all this!

JOHANSSON: We shall see! We shall certainly see!

SCENE TWO

The Round Room. In the background is a stove of gleaming white tile, and upon it are a mantelpiece clock and a candelabrum. To the right is the entrance from the hallway with a view into a Green Room furnished in mahogany. To the left is a statue shaded by palms; a curtain may be drawn to conceal it. The door upstage left leads into the Hyacinth Room in which the DAUGHTER sits reading. The COLONEL can be seen sitting in the Green Room, writing, his back to the audience. Through the entrance from the hallway come BENGTSSON, the Colonel's valet, dressed in livery, and JOHANSSON, dressed as a waiter in black tails and white tie.

BENGTSSON: You're to serve, Johansson, while I see to their coats. Have you done this before?

JOHANSSON: All day I push around his war chariot, but evenings I serve at social gatherings. I've always dreamed of getting into this house. Strange lot they have here, I must say.

BENGTSSON: Mm. Yes, you might say they're a bit—unusual.

JOHANSSON: Will it be a musical evening, or what?

BENGTSSON: No, just the run-of-the-mill ghost supper, as we call it. They drink tea but say nothing. Unless the Colonel has something. Then they nibble away at their small cakes—all in unison, mind you—sounding like mice in an attic.

JOHANSSON: Why a ghost supper?

BENGTSSON: Because they all look like ghosts. They've kept it going for twenty years. The same people saying the same things. Either that or they say nothing—to avoid making fools of themselves.

JOHANSSON: Is there a mistress of the house?

BENGTSSON: Oh, yes, but she's mad as a loon. Sits in a large closet; says her eyes can't stand the light. *(Points to a concealed, wallpapered door.)* In there.

JOHANSSON: In there?

BENGTSSON: As I said, they're a bit peculiar—

JOHANSSON: What does she look like?

BENGTSSON: Like a mummy. Want to see her? *(Opens the wallpapered door.)* There she sits!

JOHANSSON: Holy Jes—!

MUMMY: *(Babbling.)* Why are you always opening the door? I told you to keep it closed!

BENGTSSON: *(Wheedling.)* Na-na-na-na-naa! If Polly's a good girl she'll get something good. Pretty Polly!

MUMMY: *(Like a parrot.)* Pretty Polly! Is that you, Jacob? Crrrr!

BENGTSSON: She thinks she's a parrot—and she may be right. *(To the MUMMY.)* Polly want to whistle for us?

(The MUMMY whistles.)

JOHANSSON: I've seen a lot, but nothing like this.

BENGTSSON: When a house grows old, you see, it begins to molder. And when humans are together for a long time and torment one another, they go mad. This woman here—shut up, Polly!—this mummy, has lived here for forty years—with the same husband, the same furniture, the same relatives, the same friends— *(Closes the door on the MUMMY.)* And as for what's gone on in this house, I don't understand. Look at that statue. That's the mistress of the house when she was young.

JOHANSSON: My God! Is that the mummy?

BENGTSSON: Yes, and it's enough to make you want to cry. But that woman—either through her own imagination, or for other reasons—has assumed the particular speech patterns of a parrot. That's why she can't abide either the cripples or the sick in her presence—not even her own daughter, because she's sick, too.

JOHANSSON: The young lady? Sick?

BENGTSSON: You'll see soon enough.

JOHANSSON: *(Looking at the statue.)* It's horrible to think that—How old is that woman?

BENGTSSON: No one knows. But they say that when she was thirty-five she looked nineteen, and convinced the Colonel into believing it, in this very house. Do you know what that black Japanese screen there by the chaise is for? It's called the death screen. And whenever anyone's about to die, they put it around them, just like in a hospital.

JOHANSSON: What a horrible house. And to think the young student was eating his heart out to get in, like it was Paradise.

BENGTSSON: Student? Oh, that one. The one who's expected here this evening. The Colonel and the young lady met him at the opera this afternoon and were taken with him. Hm. But now it's my turn to ask questions. Who's your master? The old goat in the wheelchair?

JOHANSSON: Yes, of course.—Will he be here, too, this evening?

BENGTSSON: He hasn't been invited.

JOHANSSON: He'll come uninvited if he has to.

(The OLD MAN appears in the hallway, dressed in frock coat, top hat, and on crutches. He steals forward and listens.)

BENGTSSON: He must be a regular old rogue, eh?

JOHANSSON: Bad as they come.

BENGTSSON: He looks like the devil incarnate.

JOHANSSON: He's a magician. He walks through locked doors.

OLD MAN: *(Steps forward and takes JOHANSSON by the ear.)* Scoundrel! Take care! *(To BENGTSSON.)* You may announce me to the Colonel.

BENGTSSON: But we're expecting guests.

OLD MAN: I know that. But my visit is not unexpected—if not entirely looked forward to.

BENGTSSON: Yes, well. What name shall I announce? Mr. Hummel?

OLD MAN: Precisely! *(BENGTSSON goes through the hallway into the Green Room, closing the door behind him.)* Johansson, get out of here! *(JOHANSSON hesitates.)* Out! *(JOHANSSON disappears into the hallway. The OLD MAN inspects the room. Finally, in great astonishment, he stops in front of the statue.)* Amelia! It's she! Amelia! *(He wanders about the room, fingering things, sets his wig in order in front of the mirror, then turns again toward the statue.)*

MUMMY: *(From the closet.)* Prrr-etty Polly!

OLD MAN: *(Startled.)* What was that? Is there a parrot in the room? I don't see one.

MUMMY: Is that you, Jacob?

OLD MAN: The house is haunted!

MUMMY: Jacob!

OLD MAN: I'm afraid—! So these are the secrets they hide in this house! *(With his back to the closet, he stands looking at a portrait.)* There he is! The old Colonel himself!

MUMMY: *(Comes out of the closet and approaches the OLD MAN from behind, pulling at his wig.)* Crrr! Is it? Crrr!

OLD MAN: *(Jumps.)* Good God! Who is it?

MUMMY: *(In a natural voice.)* Is it Jacob?

OLD MAN: Yes, my name is Jacob.

MUMMY: *(Movingly.)* And my name is Amelia.

OLD MAN: No—oh, no—oh my God!

MUMMY: This is how I look! *(Pointing at the statue.)* And that's how I looked once upon a pretty time! Life teaches one to—see. I live mostly in the closet so as not to have to see and to be seen. But you, Jacob, what do you want here?

OLD MAN: My child! Our child!

MUMMY: There she is.

OLD MAN: Where?

MUMMY: There. In the Hyacinth Room.

OLD MAN: *(Looking at the DAUGHTER.)* Yes—there she is! *(Pause.)* What about her father—the Colonel, I mean—your husband?

MUMMY: I was angry with him once, and told him everything—

OLD MAN: And—?

MUMMY: He didn't believe me. He said: "That's what all wives say when they want to murder their husbands." Say what you will, it was a terrible crime. It has falsified his whole life, and even his family tree. Sometimes I look into the *Peerage*, and say to myself: Here she is, going around with a false birth certificate, like any servant girl, and they send people to the penitentiary for such things.

OLD MAN: A lot of people have them. If I recall, you falsified the date of your own birth.

MUMMY: It was my mother's fault. Not mine. But you were the one most to blame in our crime.

OLD MAN: No! It was your husband who caused the crime when he stole my fiancée from me. I was born unable to forgive until I had taken my vengeance. It was a duty I could not ignore, and I acted accordingly.

MUMMY: What are you looking for in this house? What do you want? How did you get in? Is it because of my daughter? If you touch her, you shall die!

OLD MAN: I mean her no harm!

MUMMY: Then you must spare her father!

OLD MAN: No!

MUMMY: Than you shall die! In this very room! Behind that screen.

OLD MAN: That may be. But once I set my teeth in something, I can't let loose.

MUMMY: You want to marry her to that student. Why? He *is* nothing and *has* nothing.

OLD MAN: He'll be rich—I'll make him that.

MUMMY: Were you invited here this evening?

OLD MAN: No, but I intend to invite myself to this ghost supper!

MUMMY: Do you know who's coming?

OLD MAN: Not exactly.

MUMMY: The baron from upstairs, whose father-in-law was buried this afternoon.

OLD MAN: The one getting the divorce to marry the daughter of the care-taker's wife. The man who was once—your lover.

MUMMY: And then there will be your former fiancée, who was seduced by my husband—

OLD MAN: Quite a gathering—

MUMMY: Oh, God, why can't we die! If only we could die!

OLD MAN: Why do you insist on meeting like this?

MUMMY: Guilts—secrets—crimes bind us together. We've broken with one another, we've gone our own ways, but we are always drawn back together.

OLD MAN: I think the Colonel is coming.

MUMMY: Then I'll go in to Adèle. *(Pause.)* Jacob, take care what you do! Spare him— *(Pause. She goes into the Hyacinth Room.)*

COLONEL: *(Enters, calm and reserved.)* Be seated, please. *(The OLD MAN sits down slowly. Pause. The COLONEL stares at him.)* Are you the gentleman who wrote the letter?

OLD MAN: Yes.

COLONEL: You are Mr. Hummel?

OLD MAN: Yes. *(Pause.)*

COLONEL: As I understand it, you have bought up all of my promissory notes, from which I must conclude that I am in your hands. What do you want?

OLD MAN: I want to be paid, in one way or another.

COLONEL: In what way?

OLD MAN: In a very simple way. Let's not talk about money. You have merely to bear with me in your house—as a guest.

COLONEL: If you're satisfied with so little—

OLD MAN: Oh, thank you.

COLONEL: What else?

OLD MAN: Dismiss Bengtsson!

COLONEL: But why should I do that? A trusted servant like him! He's served a lifetime in this house! He received a distinguished service medal for his service! Why should I dismiss him?

OLD MAN: Because all the virtues you mention exist only in your imagination. He's not what he appears to be.

COLONEL: Who is?

OLD MAN: *(Taken aback.)* That's true. But nonetheless, Bengtsson must be dismissed.

COLONEL: Are you to run my house for me?

OLD MAN: Yes. Since everything here belongs to me—furniture, curtains, silver, linens—and all the rest—

COLONEL: What do you mean by "all the rest"?

OLD MAN: Everything. Everything here belongs to me. My property!

COLONEL: All right! I can't argue that! Your property! But my good name, my coat of arms—are mine!

OLD MAN: No—mine. *(Pause.)* You are not a nobleman.

COLONEL: How dare you!

OLD MAN: *(Withdraws a paper.)* Read this passage from *The Book of Peerage.* You will discover that the family whose name you have assumed has been extinct for one hundred years.

COLONEL: *(Reads.)* Yes—I've heard these rumors. But I inherited my title from my father. *(Reads on.)* It's true, yes. You're quite right. I'm not of the nobility. Even that has now been stripped from me. Along with my signet ring. It's true. It's yours now. Here—

OLD MAN: *(Puts the ring in his pocket.)* We now continue. You're not a colonel, either.

COLONEL: Not a—?

OLD MAN: No. You were an acting colonel in the American Volunteer Services, but after the war with Cuba and the reorganization of the army, all such earlier titles were abolished.

COLONEL: Is this true?

OLD MAN: *(Reaching into his pocket.)* Would you care to read about it?

COLONEL: No—that won't be necessary. Who are you, that you assume the right to sit here and strip me naked in this fashion?

OLD MAN: You'll see soon enough. But as for stripping you naked—do you know who you really are?

COLONEL: How dare you!

OLD MAN: Take off your wig and look at yourself in the mirror; take out the false teeth and shave off the mustache; let Bengtsson undo your metal corset. We'll see then whether or not the servant recognizes himself, the same servant who sponged food from a certain kitchen. *(The COLONEL is about to reach for the bell on the table; the OLD MAN prevents him.)* Don't touch that bell! And don't call Bengtsson. Do so and I'll have him arrested.—Your guests are arriving. Stay calm and we'll continue playing our rôles awhile longer.

COLONEL: Who are you? I recognize those eyes, and that voice—

OLD MAN: Don't ask. Keep silent and do as you're told.

STUDENT: *(Enters and bows to the COLONEL.)* Colonel!

COLONEL: Welcome to my house, young man! Your heroism at last night's terrible disaster has put your name on everyone's lips. I consider it an honor to receive you in my house.

STUDENT: My humble origins, Colonel—your illustrious name and noble birth—

COLONEL: May I introduce you? Mr. Arkenholz, Mr. Hummel. Be so kind, Mr. Arkenholz, as to join the ladies in the other room. I have a few more words to say to Mr. Hummel. *(The STUDENT goes into the Hyacinth Room and remains visible as he speaks with the DAUGHTER.)* Splendid young man! He has an aptitude for music, sings, writes poetry. If he were a nobleman and of equal birth, I should have no objection to his—hm—

OLD MAN: To his what?

COLONEL: My daughter—

OLD MAN: *Your* daughter! Speaking of her, why does she always sit in that room?

COLONEL: A peculiarity of hers. She feels she must sit in the Hyacinth Room whenever she's at home. Ah, here comes Miss Beata von Holsteinkrona. Charming woman, a pillar of the church, with an income which precisely matches her birth and her position.

OLD MAN: *(To himself.)* My fiancée.

(The FIANCÉE enters, white-haired, and rather demented looking.)

COLONEL: Miss von Holsteinkrona, Mr. Hummel. *(The FIANCÉE nods her head and sits down. The ARISTOCRAT enters in mourning, looking mysterious. He sits down.)* Baron Skanskorg—

OLD MAN: *(Aside, without rising.)* I do believe that's the jewel thief— *(To the COLONEL.)* Let out the Mummy and our party will be complete.

COLONEL: *(At the door to the Hyacinth Room.)* Polly!

MUMMY: *(Enters.)* Crrrr! Crrrr! Crrrr!

COLONEL: Are the young people to come in, too?

OLD MAN: No. Not the young ones. Let's spare them.

(All sit silently in a circle.)

COLONEL: Shall we have some tea?

OLD MAN: Tea? Why? No one likes tea, so why pretend! *(Pause.)*

COLONEL: Then shall we talk?

OLD MAN: *(Slowly and with pauses.)* About what? The weather? But we know that. Ask how we're all doing? We know that, too. I prefer silence. In silence we see thoughts. In silence we see the past. Silence conceals nothing. Words conceal. I read recently that language differences arose among primitive savage tribes—they needed to keep tribal secrets private and unknown to rival tribes. Languages, therefore, are codes, and whoever finds the key will understand all the world's languages. Not that secrets can't be discovered without a key. Particularly in cases where proof of paternity is at issue. Legal proof, of course, is another matter. Two false witnesses testifying in court are sufficient, as long as their testimonies agree. But in such cases as I have in mind no witnesses are possible. Nature herself has endowed man with a sense of shame which attempts to hide what ought to be hidden. At times, of course, without willing it, we slip into situations, in which, at times, by chance, the most secret of secrets must be revealed, where the mask is torn from the impostor, and where the villain is exposed. *(Pause. They all look at one another in silence.)* How quiet it has become. *(Long silence.)* Here, for example, in this respectable house, in this elegant home, where wealth and culture and beauty are united. *(Long silence.)* All of us sitting here know who we are. Do we not? No need for me to tell you. And each of you knows me, although you pretend not to. And sitting in that room is my daughter—*my* daughter, yes—as you also know. She's lost her desire to live and doesn't know why. She's withered away in this air polluted with crime and deception and lies of every kind. That's why I've searched to find her a friend, a friend in whose presence she may once again experience the light and the warmth that emanate from a noble deed. *(Long silence.)* That was my aim in this house. To pull up weeds, to unmask crimes, to settle accounts, so that these young people can make a new beginning, a new life in this home, which is my gift to them. *(Long silence.)* Each of you will now depart in peace and safe conduct, and whoever stays behind will be arrested. *(Long silence.)* Listen to the ticking, ticking of the clock. Like the ticking of the deathwatch beetle in the wall. Do you hear what it says? "Time-is-up! Time-is-up!" When it strikes—in another moment—your time will be up. Then you may go—not before. But before it strikes, it threatens you. Listen! It's warning! "The clock-can-strike!" And I can strike, too! *(He strikes the table with one of his crutches.)* Do you hear? *(Silence.)*

MUMMY: *(Goes to the clock and stops it; then speaks clearly and seriously.)* But I can stop time in its course. I can undo the past, make what is done undone. But not with threats and bribes—but through suffering and repentance. *(She goes to the OLD MAN.)* We are weak and miserable creatures; we know that. We have erred, we have sinned, the same as all the others. We are not what we seem, for at bottom we are better than what we believe, because we despise and condemn our sins. But when you, Jacob Hummel, with your false name, set yourself up to judge us, you prove you are worse and more contemptible than we who are miserable! You are not who you seem to be! You are a thief of the souls of men! You once stole me with your false promises, just as you murdered the consul here we buried today, strangled him with his debts; and you stole that student's soul by binding him to you with an imaginary debt of his father's, who never owed you a cent. *(The OLD MAN has attempted to rise and speak; but he crumples back into his chair and shrinks smaller and smaller as she continues.)* But there is a dark spot in your life that I don't know the full truth of, though I have my suspicions. But I suspect Bengtsson knows. *(She rings the bell on the table.)*

OLD MAN: No! Not Bengtsson! Not him!

MUMMY: Then he *does* know! *(She rings again. The MILKMAID appears in the door to the hallway. She is visible to no one but the OLD MAN who is struck with horror. At BENGTSSON's entrance, the MILKMAID disappears.)* Bengtsson, do you know this person?

BENGTSSON: Yes, and he knows me. Life has its ups and downs, as you must know. I was in his service once and he in mine. For two whole years he sponged food from my kitchen—he was the cook's boyfriend. Since he had to leave at three, dinner had to be ready at two, so for the sake of this ox we had to be satisfied with his warmed leftovers. But he drank the soup stock, too; what was left had to be eked out with water. He sat outside like a vampire sucking the marrow from the house so that we became skeletons. And he very nearly had us thrown in jail, because we accused the cook of being a thief.—I met this man later in Hamburg. He had another name. He'd become a loan shark, a bloodsucker. It was there he was accused of having lured a young girl out onto the ice to drown her—she'd witnessed a crime he was afraid would come to light.

MUMMY: *(Passes her hand over the face of the OLD MAN.)* This is who you are! Now give me the promissory notes and your will! *(JOHANSSON appears in the door to the hallway and watches the proceedings with great interest, with the knowledge that he is about to be freed from slavery. The OLD MAN extracts the packet of papers from his pocket and throws it on the table. The MUMMY strokes the OLD MAN's back.)* Polly!—Is that you, Jacob?

OLD MAN: *(Like a parrot.)* Jacob is here! Pretty-pretty Polly!

MUMMY: Can the clock strike?

OLD MAN: The clock can strike! *(Imitating a cuckoo clock.)* Cuckoo! Cuckoo! Cuckoo!

MUMMY: *(Opening the door to the closet.)* Now the clock has struck! Get up! Go into the closet where I have sat for twenty years mourning our sin! In there you will find a rope hanging. Let it represent the rope you used to strangle the consul up there, and with which you intended to strangle your benefactor. Go! *(The OLD MAN enters the closet. The MUMMY closes the door.)* Bengtsson! Set up the screen! The death screen! *(BENGTSSON sets up the death screen in front of the door.)*

ALL. Amen!

(Long silence.—In the Hyacinth Room the DAUGHTER sits at a harp and, after a prelude, accompanies the STUDENT's recitation of a song.)

STUDENT: I saw the sun, and so it seemed
That I beheld the Hidden One
Whose works must give us joy.
Blessèd the man who works for good!
Never seek to right with evil
Deeds that you have done in anger.
Comfort whom you have afflicted,
Through kindness will the grievance heal.
Innocence is free of fear.
The innocent is blest.

SCENE THREE

The Hyacinth Room. The room is decorated in a bizarre Oriental style. Hyacinths of all colors are everywhere. On the tile stove rests a large statue of a seated Buddha, in whose lap is a bulb out of which rises the stem of an Ascalon flower that erupts into a globular cluster of white star-shaped flowers. Upstage right is the doorway to the Round Room where the COLONEL and the MUMMY sit motionless and silent. A section of the death screen is also visible. Stage left is the doorway to the pantry and kitchen. The STUDENT and the DAUGHTER are at the table; she seated at her harp, he standing beside her.

DAUGHTER: Sing for my flowers!

STUDENT: Is this your favorite flower?

DAUGHTER: Yes. Do you love the hyacinth, too?

STUDENT: More than all others. I love its delicate stalk, straight and slender as a young girl, rising from the bulb that rests on the water and sends down pure white roots into the colorless liquid. I love its colors: snow-white innocence, lovely honey-yellow, youthful pink, dark ripe red; but most of all the blue—blue of mist, deep-eyed blue, the blue of faithfulness—I love them all, more than gold and pearls. I've worshipped and loved them since childhood because they have all the virtues that I don't have. And yet—

DAUGHTER: What?

STUDENT: My love was never returned—these beautiful flowers hate me.

DAUGHTER: How?

STUDENT: Their perfume confuses my senses—like the strong, clean, first winds of spring that pass over melting snows—it deafens me, blinds me, drives me from the room, it bombards me with poison arrows that sadden my heart and enflame my mind. Don't you know the story behind this flower?

DAUGHTER: Tell me.

STUDENT: But first of all its meaning. The bulb that rests on the water or is buried in soil is the earth. And then the stalk rises up, straight as the world's axis, and at its top sit its six-pointed star-flowers.

DAUGHTER: Above the earth! Stars! Oh, how wonderful! Where did you see this vision? How did you—

STUDENT: Where? Where else? In your eyes! Don't you see? It's an image of the world—of the cosmos. That's why the Buddha sits there, the earth-bulb in his lap, his eyes brooding over it as it grows out and up and transforms itself into a heaven. This miserable earth will become a heaven! And this is what the Buddha waits for!

DAUGHTER: Yes—I see it now! And snowflakes—don't snowflakes have six points, too?

STUDENT: Of course! Because snowflakes are fallen stars!

DAUGHTER: And the snowdrop is a snow-star that has grown from snow.

STUDENT: But Sirius, the largest and most beautiful of all the stars in the firmament, is red and gold, just like the narcissus with its red and gold chalice, and its six white rays—

DAUGHTER: Have you ever seen the Ascalon in bloom?

STUDENT: Of course I have. It hides its blossoms in a ball, a globe, like the firmament strewn with white stars.

DAUGHTER: Oh, God, how wonderful! Whose vision was that?

STUDENT: Yours!

DAUGHTER: Yours!

STUDENT: Ours! Together we gave birth to a vision. And so, we're married—

DAUGHTER: Not yet—

STUDENT: What more is there?

DAUGHTER: Waiting, trials, tests of patience!

STUDENT: All right, then! Put me to the test! *(Pause.)* Tell me something. Why are your parents sitting so quietly in there, without a word?

DAUGHTER: Because they have nothing more to say to each other. And because one never believes what the other says. My father said once: "What's the sense in talking when we can't pull the wool over each other's eyes?"

STUDENT: That's horrible!

DAUGHTER: Here comes the cook. Look at her, so big and fat.

STUDENT: What does she want?

DAUGHTER: To ask about dinner. Since my mother's illness I've managed the house.

STUDENT: Then why do we have to bother about the kitchen?

DAUGHTER: We have to eat. Just look at her! I can't bear to look—

STUDENT: Who is this ogre?

DAUGHTER: She's a Hummel—that family of vampires—she's eating us up—

STUDENT: Why not dismiss her?

DAUGHTER: She won't leave! There's no controlling her. She's punishment for our sins. Can't you see how we're wasting away?

STUDENT: Doesn't she feed you?

DAUGHTER: Oh, she serves us all kinds of dishes; it's just that there's no nourishment in them. She boils the meat till it's nothing but fibers and water—and drinks the stock herself. When it's a roast, she cooks out the juices and drinks the broth. Everything she touches loses its strength—as if she sucked it out with her eyes. She drinks the coffee, we're served the dregs. She drinks the wine then fills the bottles with water.

STUDENT: Drive her out!

DAUGHTER: We can't!

STUDENT: Why not?

DAUGHTER: We don't know. She won't leave. We don't know what to do with her. She's taken all our strength.

STUDENT: Shall *I* get rid of her?

DAUGHTER: No. It's just the way it is. She has to stay. She'll come and ask what to cook for dinner; I'll make suggestions; she'll object—and then go off and do as she pleases.

STUDENT: Then let *her* decide what to cook.

DAUGHTER: She doesn't want that.

STUDENT: What a strange house. It's bewitched.

DAUGHTER: Yes.—But she's turning back now. She saw you.

COOK: *(Appears in the doorway.)* No, that wasn't why. *(She grins, showing all her teeth.)*

STUDENT: *(To the COOK.)* Get out!

COOK: When I'm good and ready! *(Pause.)* Now I'm ready. *(Goes.)*

DAUGHTER: Don't get excited. You should learn patience. She's one of the trials we have to endure. We also have a maid that we have to clean up after.

STUDENT: My head's reeling! *Cor in aethere!* Sing to me!

DAUGHTER: No, wait!

STUDENT: Music!

DAUGHTER: Be patient! This room is known as the Room of Trials. It's beautiful to look at, but it's made of pure imperfection—

STUDENT: I don't believe it! And if so, it's better to ignore them. It's a beautiful room, just a little bit cold. Why don't you light a fire?

DAUGHTER: It smokes—

STUDENT: Then have the chimney swept.

DAUGHTER: That doesn't help. Do you see that desk over there?

STUDENT: Yes, it's magnificent!

DAUGHTER: It wobbles. Every day I cut and lay a piece of cork under the short leg, but the housemaid always takes it away when she sweeps, and I have to cut a new one. Every morning the pen and inkwell are clogged; I have to clean them after she's left. Every blessèd day. *(Pause.)* What's the most disagreeable task you can think of?

STUDENT: Sorting the wash! Ugh!

DAUGHTER: That's my job, too! Ugh!

STUDENT: And what else?

DAUGHTER: To be wakened every night and latch the top window that the housemaid failed to close.

STUDENT: And what else?

DAUGHTER: To climb the ladder and tie the cord back onto the stove-damper that the housemaid broke off.

STUDENT: And what else?

DAUGHTER: To sweep up after her, dust after her, light the fire in the stove after her—all *she* does is throw in the wood. And then I tend to the damper, dry the glasses, set the table, uncork the bottles, open the windows and air the rooms, and remake my bed. I rinse out the water carafe when it's grown green with algae. I buy matches and soap that we're always running out of. I clean the chimneys of the lamps and trim the wicks so that they don't smoke. And then, so the lamps don't go out when we have guests, I have to fill them myself—

STUDENT: Sing me a song!

DAUGHTER: Wait! First comes the toil. Toil to keep the dirt of life at a distance.

STUDENT: But you're wealthy. You have two servants.

DAUGHTER: That doesn't help. Not even if we had three. Life is difficult. There are times I grow tired of it. And just imagine a house full of children as well!

STUDENT: There's no greater joy!

DAUGHTER: And none more costly! Is life worth so many troubles?

STUDENT: That depends on the reward you expect for your troubles. I wouldn't shrink from anything to win your hand.

DAUGHTER: Don't say such things. You can never have me.

STUDENT: But why?

DAUGHTER: Better not to ask. *(Pause.)*

STUDENT: You dropped your bracelet from the window—

DAUGHTER: Because my hand has grown so thin— *(Pause. The COOK appears with a Japanese bottle in her hand.)* There she is—the one who's eating me—eating us all!

STUDENT: What's that in her hand?

DAUGHTER: The bottle with coloring in it, with letters like scorpions. It's soy. She uses it to change water into stock, to make gravy, to cook cabbage in, to make turtle soup—

STUDENT: *(To the COOK.)* Get out!

COOK: You suck strength from *us*, we suck it from *you*. We take your blood and give you back water—colored water—here's the coloring! I'm leaving now, but I'll stay as long as I want. *(Goes out.)*

STUDENT: Why did Bengtsson get his medal?

DAUGHTER: For his great merits.

STUDENT: Has he no faults?

DAUGHTER: Oh, yes, very great ones. You just don't get medals for them. *(Both laugh.)*

STUDENT: You have lots of secrets in this house.

DAUGHTER: The same as in other houses. Allow us to keep ours. *(Pause.)*

STUDENT: Do you like honesty?

DAUGHTER: Yes, within reason.

STUDENT: At times I have the mad impulse to say everything I'm thinking. But I also know the world would come to a crashing end if we were all completely honest. *(Pause.)* I was at a funeral the other day—in church—very solemn, very beautiful.

DAUGHTER: Mr. Hummel's funeral?

STUDENT: Yes, my false benefactor's. At the head of the coffin stood an old friend of the deceased carrying the mace. I was especially impressed with the minister, his dignified bearing, his moving sermon. I cried. We all cried. Afterwards we went to an inn, and there I learned that the man with the mace had been in love with the dead man's son— *(The DAUGHTER stares at him searchingly, trying to understand.)*—and that the dead man had borrowed money from his son's lover. *(Pause.)* The next day, the minister was arrested for embezzlement of church funds. How's that for a pretty story!

DAUGHTER: Oh! *(Pause.)*

STUDENT: Do you know what I'm thinking about now—about you?

DAUGHTER: Don't tell me! I'll die!

STUDENT: But I have to, or *I'll* die!

DAUGHTER: In madhouses people say everything they think.

STUDENT: I know. My father died in a madhouse.

DAUGHTER: Was he ill?

STUDENT: No. He was well enough. It's just that he was crazy! It showed itself only once. I'll tell you about it. Well, like all the rest of us, he had a circle of acquaintances—he called them friends for brevity's sake. Naturally they were a herd of scoundrels, like most humans. Still, he had to have some social connections, he couldn't sit around alone all the time. Well, since one doesn't usually tell people what one thinks of them, he didn't either. And yet he knew how false they were. He'd sounded out their deceit. But being a wise man and well bred, he was always courteous. Then one day he gave a large party. It was in the evening. He was tired after the day's work. And tired also from having to keep still and talk only nonsense with his guests— *(The DAUGHTER shudders.)* Then at supper he tapped for silence, reached for his glass, and delivered a speech. All at once the locks broke and in a long speech he stripped naked the entire gathering, one after the other, and told them of all their baseness. He then sat down exhausted in the middle of the table and told them to go to hell!

DAUGHTER: Oh!

STUDENT: I was there, and I'll never forget what happened next. My mother and father came to blows, striking out at each other, the guests ran for the doors—and my father was taken to the madhouse, where he died. *(Pause.)* When water has stood still for too long it turns rotten. It's the same with people. That's how it is with this house. There's something rotten here. But when I saw you walk through that door for the first time, I thought it was Paradise. I stood there one Sunday morning looking in. I saw a colonel who wasn't a colonel. I found a benefactor who was a thief and had to hang himself. I saw a mummy who wasn't a mummy, and an innocent young girl. Where is innocence to be found? Where is beauty? In nature and flowers and trees—in my mind when I'm dressed up in my Sunday clothes! Where is honor, where is faith? In fairy tales! In children's games! Where is anything to be found that fulfills its promise? In my imagination. Your flowers have poisoned me, and I've poisoned you in return. I asked you to become my wife and to make a home with me. We recited poetry, we sang, we played. And then the cook entered. *Sursum corda!* Try once more to strike fire and glory from your golden harp! Try! I beg you! I implore you on my knees! Well—then I'll do it myself. *(He takes the harp but the strings fail to sound.)* It's deaf and dumb! Why should the most beautiful flowers be the most poisonous? It's a curse—all creation is damned—all life is damned. Why didn't you want to be my bride? Because your life is poisoned to its core. I can feel that vampire in the kitchen beginning to suck my blood. She's a demon who sucks the blood of children. It's always in the kitchen that children are nipped in the bud—unless it's happened before in the bedroom. There are poisons that blind, and poisons that open the eyes. I was born with the second. My eyes are open. I see no beauty in ugliness. I can call no evil good. I can't! They say that Jesus harrowed hell. What they mean is He descended to this madhouse, this prison, this charnel house that we call earth! And the madmen He came to free murdered Him! Only the thief was freed! A thief always gets the sympathy. Alas for us all! Alas! Savior of the world, save us, we perish!

(The DAUGHTER has collapsed and appears to be dying. She rings the bell. BENGTSSON enters.)

DAUGHTER: Bring the screen. Quickly! I'm dying.

(BENGTSSON returns with the screen, opens it, and places it in front of the DAUGHTER.)

STUDENT: The Deliverer is coming! Welcome, pale and gentle Spirit! And

you, lovely, doomed, innocent creature, blameless in your suffering—
sleep—sleep a dreamless sleep. And when you wake—may you be
greeted by a sun that doesn't burn, in a home without dust, by friends
without faults, and by a love that knows no stain.—Wise and gentle
Buddha, you who sit there waiting for a heaven to rise out of earth, grant
us patience in our trials, and purity of will, that your hope will not come
to nothing!
*(The strings of the harp begin to murmur softly and the room is filled with
a white light.)*

STUDENT: I saw the sun, and so it seemed
That I beheld the Hidden One
Whose works must give us joy.
Blessèd the man who works for good!
Never seek to right with evil
Deeds that you have done in anger.
Comfort whom you have afflicted,
Through kindness will the grievance heal.
Innocence is free of fear.
The innocent is blest.
(A soft moaning is heard from behind the screen.)

STUDENT: Poor, dear child, child of this world of delusion, of guilt, suffering, and of death; this world of eternal change, of disappointment,
and of pain! May the Lord of Heaven be merciful to you on your journey—
*(The room disappears. In the distance Böcklin's painting "The Isle of the
Dead" is seen. From the island we hear soft, pleasant, melancholy music.)*

END OF PLAY

A LIST FOR FURTHER READING

Antoine, André. *Memories of the Théâtre Libre.* Coral Gables: 1964.

Brandell, Gunnar. *Strindberg in Inferno.* Cambridge: 1974.

Carter, Lawson A. *Zola and the Theatre.* New Haven: 1963.

Lamm, Martin. *August Strindberg.* New York: 1971.

Marker, Lise-Lone. *The Scandinavian Theatre: A Short History.* Oxford: 1975.

Meyer, Michael. *Strindberg.* New York: 1985.

Sprigge, Elizabeth. *The Strange Life of August Strindberg.* New York: 1949.

Strindberg, August. *From an Occult Diary.* New York: 1965.

——————. *Letters of Strindberg to Harriet Bosse.* New York: 1959.

——————. *Open Letters to the Intimate Theater.* Seattle: 1966.

Valency, Maurice. *The Flower and the Castle: An Introduction to Modern Drama.* New York: 1963.

Waxman, S. M. *Antoine and the Théâtre Libre.* Cambridge: 1926.

CARL R. MUELLER has since 1967 been a professor of theater at UCLA. He has won many awards, including the Samuel Goldwyn Award for Dramatic Writing, and in 1960–61 was a Fulbright Scholar in Berlin. A translator for almost forty years, he has translated and published works by Büchner, Brecht, Wedekind, Hauptmann, Hofmannsthal, Hebbel, and Zuckmayer among many others. His most recent volume for Smith and Kraus is *Arthur Schnitzler: Four Major Plays,* published in 1999. Mr. Mueller is also the co-translator of the complete plays of Sophocles which will soon be published. His translations have been staged in every part of the English-speaking world.